Better Homes and Gardens®

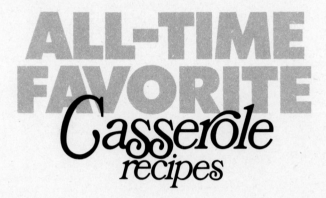

ALL-TIME FAVORITE Casserole recipes

First Edition. Eleventh Printing, 1980.
Library of Congress Catalog Card Number: 76-19685
ISBN: 0-696-00095-4

On the cover: Attractive, tasty casseroles
are always welcome at mealtime. Look
what they can do: *Round Steak Louisiana* (see
recipe, page 16) satisfies the heartiest
of appetites; *Green Beans Parmesan* (see
recipe, page 86) rounds out any menu
with good nutrition; and *Ham and Vegetables
Mornay* (see recipe, page 34) makes a
party dish from leftover ham. But this is
just a sampling of the delicious casseroles
you'll discover as you leaf through
the pages that follow, so don't stop here!

BETTER HOMES AND GARDENS® BOOKS

Editorial Director: Don Dooley
Executive Editor: Gerald Knox
Art Director: Ernest Shelton
Assistant Art Director: Randall Yontz
Production and Copy Chief: Lawrence D. Clayton
Food Editor: Doris Eby
Senior Associate Food Editor: Nancy Morton
Senior Food Editors: Sharyl Heiken,
    Elizabeth Strait
Associate Food Editors: Flora Szatkowski,
    Sandra Granseth, Diane Nelson
Graphic Designers: Harijs Priekulis,
    Faith Berven, Sheryl Veenschoten

Contents

COUNT ON A CASSEROLE

For a family meal or a gala celebration—
for an intimate twosome or two dozen—
for a quick meal or an international adventure—
let casseroles help you answer the question
"What's for dinner tonight?" There's
one for every occasion; some speed meal
preparation, some help you balance your
budget, and others are simply good eating. But
each lets you out of the kitchen while it bakes.
And you can depend on the casseroles in this
book to be the best you can find anywhere
because these are much-requested favorites from
Better Homes and Gardens.

When menus start to look the same week after week, add zest with a new casserole. Start with *Club Chicken Casserole, Tetrazzini Crepes, Pizza Siciliana, Pork Chop Supper,* and *Asparagus-Egg Casserole* (see index for page numbers), then explore the book for other exciting ideas.

1 For the Family

A casserole to fit your daily needs—that's what this chapter offers. First, casseroles with the special appeal that makes them family favorites. Then, several pages of quick-to-fix main dishes to help you through your busiest days (and microwave tips to shorten a number of preparation steps). And finally, some choice uses for leftovers, including two pages of exciting recipes that help you creatively use whatever foods you happen to have on hand.

Hearty casseroles featuring family-pleasing ingredients—*Sunday Chicken-Rice Bake*, *Biscuit-Topped Stew* made with leftovers (see page 43), and *Tuna Salad Bake* (see page 29).

Home-Style Casseroles

Sunday Chicken-Rice Bake

1 10¾-ounce can condensed
   cream of mushroom soup
1 cup milk
1 envelope onion soup mix
1 3-ounce can chopped
   mushrooms
1 cup regular rice
1 10-ounce package frozen peas
   and carrots, thawed
1 2½- to 3-pound ready-to-cook
   broiler-fryer chicken, cut up
  Paprika

In bowl stir together mushroom soup, milk, dry onion soup mix, and undrained mushrooms. Reserve ½ cup of the soup mixture and set aside. Stir uncooked rice and thawed vegetables into remaining soup mixture.

Turn rice mixture into a 12x7½x2-inch baking dish; arrange chicken pieces atop. Pour reserved soup mixture over chicken. Sprinkle chicken pieces with paprika. Cover tightly with foil. Bake at 375° till rice is tender, 1¼ to 1½ hours. Makes 4 to 6 servings.

Popover Chicken Tarragon

1 2½- to 3-pound ready-to-cook
   broiler-fryer chicken,
   cut up
2 tablespoons cooking oil
3 eggs
1½ cups milk
1 tablespoon cooking oil
1½ cups all-purpose flour
¾ teaspoon salt
¾ to 1 teaspoon dried tarragon,
   crushed
1 10¾-ounce can condensed
   cream of chicken soup
⅓ cup milk
1 4-ounce can mushroom stems
   and pieces, drained
2 tablespoons snipped parsley

Brown chicken pieces in the 2 tablespoons hot oil; season with a little salt and pepper. Place chicken pieces in a well-greased 13x9x2-inch baking dish.

In mixing bowl beat eggs; blend in the 1½ cups milk and the 1 tablespoon oil. Stir together flour, salt, and tarragon. Add to egg mixture; beat till smooth. Pour over chicken. Bake, uncovered, at 350° till done, 55 to 60 minutes.

Meanwhile, in saucepan stir together soup, the ⅓ cup milk, mushrooms, and parsley. Heat through, stirring occasionally. Pass sauce with chicken. Makes 4 servings.

Chicken and Onion Bake

1 2½- to 3-pound ready-to-cook
   broiler-fryer chicken,
   cut up
1 10¾-ounce can condensed
   cream of chicken soup
1 tablespoon snipped parsley
½ teaspoon poultry seasoning
1½ cups frozen small whole
   onions
  Paprika

Place chicken pieces, skin side up, in a 12x7½x2-inch baking dish. Stir together soup, parsley, and poultry seasoning; stir in onions. Spoon over chicken. Bake, covered, at 350° till chicken is tender, about 1 hour. Stir sauce; sprinkle with paprika. Serve with mashed potatoes or hot cooked rice, if desired. Makes 4 servings.

Microwave cooking directions: Cut large pieces of chicken in half. In a 12x7½x2-inch nonmetal baking dish combine soup, parsley, and poultry seasoning; stir in onions. Place chicken, skin side down, in sauce. Turn skin side up, coating with sauce. Cook, covered, in a countertop microwave oven till chicken is tender, about 25 minutes, rearranging chicken and stirring sauce every 10 minutes. Stir sauce again before serving; sprinkle with paprika.

Chicken-Spaghetti Bake

4   **ounces spaghetti**
3   **slices bacon, chopped**
½   **cup chopped onion**
1   **clove garlic, minced**
3   **tablespoons all-purpose flour**
1   **16-ounce can tomatoes, cut up**
1   **10¾-ounce can condensed cream of mushroom soup**
½   **cup milk**
1   **cup shredded American cheese (4 ounces)**
2   **cups cubed cooked chicken**
1   **10-ounce package frozen peas, thawed**
¼   **cup grated Parmesan cheese**

Break spaghetti pieces in half. Cook according to package directions; drain (should have about 2 cups).

In large saucepan cook bacon, onion, and garlic till bacon is crisp; blend in flour. Add undrained tomatoes, soup, and milk. Cook and stir till thickened and bubbly. Add shredded American cheese; stir till melted. Stir in cooked spaghetti, cubed chicken, and thawed peas.

Turn into a 2½-quart casserole; top with Parmesan. Bake, uncovered, at 350° for 45 minutes. Makes 8 servings.

Potato-Ham Scallop

2   **cups cubed fully cooked ham**
6   **to 8 medium potatoes, peeled and thinly sliced (6 cups)**
¼   **cup finely chopped onion**
⅓   **cup all-purpose flour**
2   **cups milk**
3   **tablespoons fine dry bread crumbs**
1   **tablespoon butter *or* margarine, melted**
2   **tablespoons finely snipped parsley**

Place *half* the ham in a 2-quart casserole. Cover with *half* the potatoes and *half* the onion. Sift *half* the flour over; season with salt and pepper. Repeat layering ham, potatoes, and onion. Season with additional salt and pepper. Sift remaining flour atop. Pour milk over all.

Bake, covered, at 350° till potatoes are nearly tender, 1 to 1¼ hours. Uncover. Combine bread crumbs and melted butter; sprinkle atop casserole. Top with parsley. Bake 15 minutes longer. Makes 4 to 6 servings.

Ham and Mac Bake

3½   **ounces elbow macaroni (1 cup)**
¼   **cup butter *or* margarine**
¼   **cup all-purpose flour**
2   **tablespoons brown sugar**
2   **tablespoons prepared mustard**
¼   **teaspoon salt**
     Dash pepper
2   **cups milk**
2   **cups cubed fully cooked ham**
2   **medium apples, peeled and thinly sliced (2 cups)**
1½   **cups soft bread crumbs (2 slices)**
2   **tablespoons butter *or* margarine, melted**

Cook macaroni in boiling salted water just till tender, 8 to 10 minutes; drain. In large saucepan melt the ¼ cup butter; blend in flour, brown sugar, mustard, salt, and pepper. Add milk all at once; cook and stir till thickened and bubbly. Stir in cooked macaroni, ham, and apple slices. Turn mixture into a 2-quart casserole.

Combine bread crumbs and the 2 tablespoons melted butter; sprinkle over casserole. Bake, uncovered, at 350° for about 35 minutes. Makes 6 servings.

Pork Chop-Fried Rice Casserole

1¾ cups water
1½ cups Minute Rice
 2 slices bacon
 2 beaten eggs
 2 tablespoons water
 ¼ cup sliced green onion
   with tops
 3 tablespoons soy sauce
 4 pork rib chops
   Soy sauce

In saucepan bring the 1¾ cups water to boiling. Remove from heat; stir in rice. Cover; set aside. In skillet cook bacon till crisp. Remove bacon and crumble, reserving 2 tablespoons drippings. Set aside.

In bowl combine eggs and the 2 tablespoons water. In skillet cook eggs in *1 tablespoon* of the reserved drippings till set, stirring occasionally. Cut eggs in narrow strips. Add rice, bacon, onion, and the 3 tablespoons soy sauce to eggs; mix well. Turn into a greased 1½-quart casserole.

In skillet brown chops on both sides in remaining 1 tablespoon drippings. Arrange chops atop rice mixture; brush with additional soy sauce. Bake, covered, at 350° till chops are tender, about 40 minutes. Makes 4 servings.

Microwave cooking directions: In a 1-quart glass bowl heat the 1¾ cups water, covered, in a countertop microwave oven till boiling, 4 minutes. Stir in rice. Cover; set aside.

Place bacon in a 10x6x2-inch nonmetal baking dish; cover with paper toweling. Micro-cook till crisp, 1½ to 1¾ minutes. Crumble bacon; set aside. Reserve 1 tablespoon bacon drippings in baking dish.

In glass bowl combine eggs and the 2 tablespoons water. Micro-cook till eggs puff, 1½ minutes; cut into narrow strips. Into reserved drippings stir rice, bacon, eggs, onion, and the 3 tablespoons soy sauce. Arrange chops atop rice mixture; brush with additional soy sauce.

Micro-cook, covered, for 5 minutes. Turn chops; micro-cook till chops are done, about 6 minutes.

Sweet-Sour Kraut and Chops

 4 medium baking potatoes, peeled
   and thinly sliced (4 cups)
 ½ cup chopped onion
 6 pork rib chops,
   cut ¾ inch thick
 2 tablespoons cooking oil
 1 27-ounce can sauerkraut,
   rinsed and drained
 1 20-ounce can crushed pineapple
 2 tablespoons brown sugar
 ½ teaspoon salt
   Dash pepper

In a 12x7½x2-inch baking dish combine potato slices and onion. Add ¼ cup water. Bake, covered, at 350° till nearly tender, about 45 minutes.

Meanwhile, in a skillet brown pork chops on both sides in hot oil. In bowl combine sauerkraut, undrained pineapple, and brown sugar; spoon over potato mixture. Place chops atop. Season with salt and pepper. Bake, covered, 45 minutes longer. Makes 6 servings.

Use Your Oven Wisely

Save both energy and money by planning to bake foods together that require the same oven temperature. For example, when cooking a main dish casserole or a roast, bake potatoes or other vegetables, a bread, or a dessert to serve at the same meal or even for the following day. Avoid overcrowding the oven, though, or cooking may be uneven. And check for doneness before removing from the oven, as some foods will require additional baking time.

Frank Tamale Pie

1 cup chopped onion
½ cup chopped green pepper
2 tablespoons butter
½ pound frankfurters (4 or 5)
1 16-ounce can pork and beans
   in tomato sauce
1 12-ounce can whole kernel
   corn, drained
1 8-ounce can tomato sauce
¼ cup chopped pitted ripe olives
1 clove garlic, minced
1 tablespoon sugar
2 to 3 teaspoons chili powder
1½ cups shredded American cheese
¾ cup yellow cornmeal

In a large skillet cook onion and green pepper in butter till tender but not brown.

Cut franks in ½-inch pieces. Stir into skillet along with beans, corn, tomato sauce, olives, garlic, sugar, chili powder, and dash pepper. Simmer, uncovered, till thickened, about 30 minutes. Add cheese; stir till melted. Turn mixture into a greased 12x7½x2-inch baking dish.

Place 2 cups cold water in saucepan. Stir in cornmeal and ½ teaspoon salt. Cook and stir till very thick (½ to 1 minute after mixture comes to boiling). Spoon over *hot* frank mixture, forming a lattice design as shown in photo at right. Bake, uncovered, at 375° for about 25 minutes. Makes 6 to 8 servings.

Frank-Vegetable Bake

½ cup yellow cornmeal
½ cup all-purpose flour
1 tablespoon sugar
1½ teaspoons baking powder
½ teaspoon salt
1 beaten egg
⅓ cup milk
4 tablespoons cooking oil
½ cup chopped carrot
¼ cup chopped onion
¼ cup chopped green pepper
¼ cup chopped celery
1 11½-ounce can condensed bean
   with bacon soup
¾ cup milk
2 teaspoons prepared mustard
1 pound frankfurters, sliced

Stir together cornmeal, flour, sugar, baking powder, and salt. Combine egg, the ⅓ cup milk, and *2 tablespoons* of the cooking oil. Add to dry ingredients; beat smooth.

In saucepan heat remaining 2 tablespoons oil; add vegetables. Cook, covered, 10 minutes. Blend in soup, the ¾ cup milk, and mustard; stir in franks. Bring to boiling. Turn into a 2-quart casserole. Spoon batter atop *hot* mixture. Bake, uncovered, at 425° for 20 to 25 minutes. Serves 6.

Microwave cooking directions: Prepare cornmeal batter as above. In a 2-quart glass casserole combine remaining 2 tablespoons oil and vegetables. Cook, covered, in a counter-top microwave oven till crisp-tender, 4 minutes, stirring once. Stir in soup, the ¾ cup milk, and mustard; stir in franks. Micro-cook, covered, till bubbly, 9 to 10 minutes, stirring 3 times. Drop spoonfuls of batter in a ring atop *hot* mixture; cook, uncovered, till topping is done, about 5 minutes; give dish a quarter turn every 2 minutes.

Frankfurter-Cheese Casserole

¾ cup macaroni
6 frankfurters
⅓ cup chopped onion
⅓ cup chopped green pepper
2 tablespoons butter
3 tablespoons all-purpose flour
1 teaspoon Worcestershire sauce
½ teaspoon prepared mustard
1 cup milk
1½ cups cream-style cottage
   cheese (12 ounces)

Cook macaroni according to package directions; drain well. Thinly slice *four* of the frankfurters; set aside.

Cook onion and green pepper in butter till tender but not brown. Blend in flour, Worcestershire, mustard, ¼ teaspoon salt, and dash pepper; add milk all at once. Cook and stir till thickened and bubbly. Stir in the sliced franks, cooked macaroni, and cottage cheese; mix well.

Turn into a 1½-quart casserole. Bake, uncovered, at 350° for 20 minutes, stirring once. Cut remaining 2 franks diagonally into thirds; arrange atop casserole. Bake till heated through, 15 minutes more. Makes 6 servings.

Sporting a cornmeal topper in a lattice design, *Frank Tamale Pie* offers south-of-the-border flavor in a one-dish meal. Vary the amount of chili powder to suit family preferences.

Hot Frank and Rice Salad

¾ **cup regular rice**
1½ **cups chicken broth**
2 **tablespoons butter *or***
   margarine
2 **tablespoons all-purpose flour**
2 **tablespoons prepared mustard**
2 **teaspoons sugar**
⅛ **teaspoon pepper**
1 **cup chicken broth**
1 **pound frankfurters, cut in**
   1-inch pieces (8 to 10)
4 **slices bacon, crisp-cooked,**
   drained, and crumbled
½ **cup chopped celery**
½ **cup sliced pitted ripe olives**
¼ **cup sliced green onion**
   with tops
¼ **cup sweet pickle relish**

In a saucepan prepare rice according to package directions, *except* substitute the 1½ cups chicken broth for the water and omit the salt.

In small saucepan melt butter or margarine; blend in flour, mustard, sugar, and pepper. Add the 1 cup chicken broth all at once; cook and stir till thickened and bubbly. Stir into rice with franks, bacon, celery, olives, onion, and pickle relish. Turn into a 2-quart casserole.

Bake, uncovered, at 375° till mixture is heated through, about 30 minutes. Garnish with more bacon and sliced pitted ripe olives, if desired. Makes 6 servings.

Salami-Cheese Pie

   Plain Pastry (see below)
1 **tablespoon all-purpose flour**
⅛ **teaspoon pepper**
1 **cup evaporated milk**
½ **cup shredded American cheese**
   (2 ounces)
½ **pound salami, chopped**
   (1½ cups)
1 **cup cubed cooked potato**
¼ **cup chopped onion**
2 **tablespoons chopped**
   pimiento

Prepare Plain Pastry for a single-crust pie. Prick bottom and sides well with fork. Reroll trimmings; cut with decorative cutter for pie top. Place cutouts on baking sheet. Bake cutouts and pie shell at 400°, 5 minutes for cutouts and 10 minutes for pie shell. Remove from oven; set aside. Reduce oven temperature to 350°.

In saucepan combine flour and pepper; blend in milk. Cook and stir till thickened and bubbly; remove from heat. Stir in cheese till melted. Stir in salami, potato, onion, and pimiento. Turn into pie shell; top with baked cutouts.

Bake at 350° till center is nearly set, 35 to 40 minutes. Let stand 5 minutes. Makes 6 servings.

Plain Pastry (enough for one 9-inch piecrust)

1 **cup all-purpose flour**
½ **teaspoon salt**
⅓ **cup shortening**
3 **to 4 tablespoons cold water**

Stir together flour and salt; cut in shortening till pieces are the size of small peas. Sprinkle *1 tablespoon* water over part of the mixture. Gently toss with fork; push to side of bowl. Repeat till all is moistened. Form dough into a ball. Continue as directed in recipe.

For single-crust pie: Flatten dough on lightly floured surface. Roll from center to edge till ⅛ inch thick. Fit pastry circle into a 9-inch pie plate. Trim ½ to 1 inch beyond edge of pie plate. Fold under and flute edge. Continue as directed in recipe.

For double-crust pie: Prepare dough as directed above, *except* double the recipe. Form into two balls. Flatten each ball on a lightly floured surface. Roll each from center to edge till ⅛ inch thick. Fit one pastry circle into a 9-inch pie plate. Trim crust even with rim of plate. Continue as directed in recipe.

Puffed Potatoes and Sausage

¼ cup sliced green onion
    with tops
2 tablespoons butter *or*
    margarine
3 medium potatoes,
    peeled and cubed
    (1 pound)
1 cup shredded American
    cheese (4 ounces)
3 egg yolks
⅓ cup milk
½ teaspoon salt
3 stiffly beaten
    egg whites
1 8-ounce package
    brown-and-serve
    sausage links

Cook onion in butter or margarine till tender but not brown. Cook potatoes in boiling salted water till tender, about 10 minutes; drain and mash (should have about 2 cups mashed). Beat in cooked onion and cheese.

Beat together egg yolks, milk, and salt; blend into potato mixture. Fold in beaten egg whites.

Turn into a 2-quart casserole. Arrange sausage links over potato mixture. Bake, uncovered, at 375° till set, about 45 minutes. Makes 4 or 5 servings.

Lamb-Lentil Stew

1 pound boneless lamb shoulder,
    cut in ½-inch cubes
2 tablespoons cooking oil
4 medium carrots, thinly sliced
    (2 cups)
1½ cups chopped onion
1 cup chopped celery
1 cup dry lentils
    (8 ounces)
1 tablespoon instant chicken
    bouillon granules
3 cloves garlic, minced
2 bay leaves
1 teaspoon dried oregano,
    crushed
½ teaspoon salt
⅛ teaspoon pepper
3 cups hot water

In large skillet brown lamb cubes in hot oil; drain off fat. Stir in carrots, onion, celery, lentils, bouillon granules, garlic, bay leaves, oregano, salt, and pepper.

Turn mixture into a 2- or 2½-quart casserole; add hot water. Bake, covered, at 350° till meat and vegetables are tender, about 1¾ hours, stirring once or twice. Add more water during cooking, if needed. Makes 6 servings.

Yankee Bacon Bake

½ pound sliced bacon
½ cup yellow cornmeal
1 cup milk
½ cup all-purpose flour
1 tablespoon sugar
1 teaspoon baking powder
½ teaspoon salt
1 cup milk
3 beaten egg yolks
3 stiffly beaten
    egg whites

Cook bacon till crisp; drain and coarsely crumble. Set bacon aside. In saucepan stir cornmeal into the 1 cup milk; cook, stirring constantly, till mixture is thickened and bubbly. Remove from heat.

Stir together flour, sugar, baking powder, and salt; blend into cornmeal mixture. Stir in the remaining 1 cup milk and egg yolks; fold in the beaten egg whites and crumbled bacon. Turn into a greased 1½-quart casserole or soufflé dish. Bake, uncovered, at 325° for 55 to 60 minutes. Makes 6 servings.

Beef Stew Bake

1½ pounds beef stew meat, cut in
     1-inch cubes
  2 tablespoons cooking oil
  1 10½-ounce can mushroom gravy
  1 cup tomato juice
 ½ cup water
 ½ envelope onion soup mix
     (¼ cup)
  1 teaspoon prepared horseradish
  4 medium potatoes,
     peeled and quartered
     (1¼ pounds)

In a heavy skillet brown meat in hot oil; drain off excess fat. Combine gravy, tomato juice, water, soup mix, and horseradish; stir into meat. Simmer, covered, 5 minutes.

Place potatoes in a 2-quart casserole. Top with meat mixture. Bake, covered, at 350° till meat and potatoes are tender, 1½ to 1¾ hours, stirring once or twice during baking. Makes 6 servings.

Zippy Mostaccioli

  1 pound beef chuck blade roast,
     cut in 1-inch cubes
  1 tablespoon shortening
  1 16-ounce can tomatoes, cut up
  2 carrots, halved lengthwise,
     then cut crosswise into
     1-inch pieces
 ½ cup sliced celery
 ½ cup coarsely chopped onion
1½ teaspoons salt
  1 teaspoon paprika
 ½ teaspoon chili powder
 ⅛ teaspoon pepper
1½ cups water
  3 ounces mostaccioli
     (1 cup)

In large skillet brown meat in hot shortening. Add undrained tomatoes, carrots, celery, onion, salt, paprika, chili powder, and pepper. Cover; cook over low heat 30 minutes.

Stir in water and uncooked mostaccioli. Bring to boiling. Turn into a 2-quart casserole. Bake, covered, at 350° till mostaccioli and meat are tender, 40 to 45 minutes, stirring occasionally. Makes 4 to 6 servings.

Layered Corned Beef Bake

  4 medium potatoes, peeled and
     sliced ¼ inch thick
     (4 cups)
  4 cups coarsely shredded
     cabbage
  3 tablespoons butter *or*
     margarine
  2 tablespoons all-purpose flour
 ¼ teaspoon salt
1¼ cups milk
  2 tablespoons Dijon-style
     mustard
  1 12-ounce can corned beef,
     chilled and sliced
     Paprika

Cook potato slices, covered, in large amount of boiling salted water till nearly tender, about 15 minutes. Add cabbage; cook 5 minutes more. Drain; set aside.

In saucepan melt butter; blend in flour and salt. Add milk all at once; cook and stir till thickened and bubbly. Remove from heat; stir in mustard. Add drained potatoes and cabbage; mix well.

Turn *half* of the vegetable mixture into a 2-quart casserole; top with corned beef slices. Spoon remaining vegetable mixture over all. Bake, covered, at 350° till casserole is heated through, 25 to 30 minutes. Sprinkle with paprika, if desired. Makes 6 servings.

Two-layered *Cheesy Hash-Spinach Pie* is tasty as well as thrifty. Lined with corned beef hash, the pastry boasts a colorful spinach, mushroom soup, cheese, and pimiento filling.

Cheesy Hash-Spinach Pie

Plain Pastry (see page 12)
2 10-ounce packages frozen
  chopped spinach
2 beaten eggs
1 10¾-ounce can condensed
  cream of mushroom soup
¼ cup all-purpose flour
1 tablespoon prepared
  horseradish
1 teaspoon prepared mustard
1 15-ounce can corned beef hash
1 cup shredded American cheese
  (4 ounces)
2 tablespoons chopped
  pimiento

Prepare Plain Pastry for a single-crust pie. Prick bottom and sides well with fork. Bake at 450° for 10 to 12 minutes. Remove from oven; reduce oven temperature to 350°.

Cook spinach according to package directions, *except* omit salt. Drain well, pressing out excess water. Combine eggs, mushroom soup, flour, horseradish, and mustard; stir in drained spinach.

Spread hash in baked pastry shell; spoon spinach mixture over. Bake, uncovered, at 350° for 45 minutes. Combine cheese and pimiento; sprinkle over pie. Bake 2 to 3 minutes longer. Let stand 5 minutes. Makes 6 servings.

Round Steak Louisiana (pictured on the cover)

4 **medium sweet potatoes** *or* **yams, peeled and cut ¾ inch thick**
1 **large onion, sliced**
1 **medium green pepper, cut in wedges**
1½ **pounds beef round steak, cut about ¾ inch thick**
  Salt
2 **tablespoons cooking oil**
1 **clove garlic, minced**
3 **tablespoons all-purpose flour**
1 **16-ounce can tomatoes, cut up**
½ **cup beef broth**
1 **teaspoon sugar**
½ **teaspoon salt**
½ **teaspoon dried thyme, crushed**
⅛ **teaspoon pepper**
  Several dashes bottled hot pepper sauce

Layer sweet potato slices, onion slices, and green pepper wedges in a 2-quart casserole. Cut meat in 6 serving-size pieces; pound to about half the original thickness. Sprinkle with a little salt. In skillet quickly brown meat in hot oil. Transfer meat to casserole atop sweet potato mixture; reserve drippings in skillet.

Cook garlic in reserved drippings till tender but not brown. Blend in flour. Add undrained tomatoes, beef broth, sugar, the ½ teaspoon salt, thyme, pepper, and hot pepper sauce. Cook and stir till thickened and bubbly; pour over meat and vegetables in casserole.

Bake, covered, at 350° till meat and vegetables are tender, about 1½ hours; occasionally spoon sauce over meat and vegetables. Makes 6 servings.

Stuffed Cabbage Rolls

1 **beaten egg**
½ **cup milk**
¼ **cup finely chopped onion**
1 **teaspoon Worcestershire sauce**
¾ **teaspoon salt**
  Dash pepper
1 **pound ground beef** *or*
  ½ **pound ground beef and**
  ½ **pound ground pork**
¾ **cup cooked rice**
6 **large** *or* **12 medium cabbage leaves**
1 **10¾-ounce can condensed tomato soup**
1 **tablespoon brown sugar**
1 **tablespoon lemon juice**

In mixing bowl combine egg, milk, onion, Worcestershire sauce, salt, and pepper; mix well. Add ground meat and cooked rice; mix thoroughly.

Remove center vein of cabbage leaves, keeping each leaf in one piece. Immerse leaves in boiling water till limp, about 3 minutes; drain. Place ½ cup meat mixture on each large leaf *or* ¼ cup mixture on each medium leaf; fold in sides. Starting at unfolded edge, roll up each leaf making sure folded sides are included in roll. Arrange in a 12x7½x2-inch baking dish.

Stir together condensed tomato soup, brown sugar, and lemon juice; pour sauce mixture over cabbage rolls. Bake, uncovered, at 350° for 1¼ hours, basting once or twice with sauce. Makes 6 servings.

Oven-Baked Beef-Lima Stew

1 **cup large dry lima beans**
¼ **cup all-purpose flour**
1 **8-ounce can tomatoes, cut up**
1 **cup sliced celery**
1 **cup sliced carrot**
½ **cup chopped onion**
1½ **teaspoons salt**
¼ **teaspoon Worcestershire sauce**
1 **bay leaf**
1 **pound ground beef**

Place beans in a large saucepan or Dutch oven; add 4½ cups water. Soak overnight. (Or, bring beans to boiling; reduce heat and simmer 2 minutes. Remove from heat; cover and let stand 1 hour.) *Do not drain.* Blend ½ cup cold water slowly into flour; stir into beans. Cook and stir till bubbly.

Stir in undrained tomatoes, celery, carrot, onion, salt, Worcestershire, and bay leaf. Crumble ground beef into beans. Bring mixture to boiling. (If desired, turn into a 2½-quart casserole.) Bake, covered, at 350° for about 1½ hours, stirring occasionally.

Discard bay leaf. Skim off fat. Season to taste with additional salt and pepper. Makes 6 servings.

Hamburger Pie

1 **pound ground beef**
½ **cup chopped onion**
1 **15½-ounce can cut green beans, drained**
1 **10¾-ounce can condensed tomato soup**
¼ **cup water**
¾ **teaspoon salt**
⅛ **teaspoon pepper**
3 **medium potatoes, peeled and quartered (1 pound)***
1 **beaten egg**
 Milk
½ **cup shredded American cheese (2 ounces)**

In large skillet cook meat and onion till meat is lightly browned and onion is tender; drain off fat. Stir in green beans, tomato soup, water, salt, and pepper; turn mixture into a 1½-quart casserole.

Cook potatoes in boiling salted water till tender, about 20 minutes; drain. Mash potatoes while hot; blend in egg. Add enough milk to make potatoes fluffy, yet stiff enough to hold their shape. Season to taste with salt and pepper.

Drop potatoes in mounds atop meat mixture. Sprinkle with cheese. Bake, uncovered, at 350° till heated through, 25 to 30 minutes. Makes 4 to 6 servings.

*Or prepare packaged instant mashed potatoes (enough for 4 servings) according to package directions, *except* omit the milk. Add 1 beaten egg; stir in a little milk, if necessary, to make potatoes fluffy, yet stiff enough to hold their shape. Season to taste with salt and pepper.

Spaghetti Pie

6 **ounces spaghetti**
2 **tablespoons butter** *or* **margarine**
2 **beaten eggs**
⅓ **cup grated Parmesan cheese**
1 **cup cream-style cottage cheese (8 ounces)**
1 **pound ground beef** *or* **bulk pork sausage**
½ **cup chopped onion**
¼ **cup chopped green pepper**
1 **8-ounce can tomatoes, cut up**
1 **6-ounce can tomato paste**
1 **teaspoon sugar**
1 **teaspoon dried oregano, crushed**
½ **teaspoon garlic salt**
½ **cup shredded mozzarella cheese (2 ounces)**

Cook spaghetti according to package directions; drain (should have about 3 cups). Stir butter or margarine into hot spaghetti; stir in beaten eggs and Parmesan cheese. Form spaghetti mixture into a "crust" in a greased 10-inch pie plate. Spread with cottage cheese.

In skillet cook ground meat, onion, and green pepper till meat is brown and vegetables are tender. Drain off fat. Stir in undrained tomatoes, tomato paste, sugar, oregano, and garlic salt; heat through.

Turn meat mixture into spaghetti crust. Bake, uncovered, at 350° for 20 minutes. Sprinkle with mozzarella cheese; bake till melted, about 5 minutes. Makes 6 servings.

Containers for Casseroles

The wrong baking container can ruin a good casserole. So, for best results, use the dish the recipe recommends. If you do substitute, remember that food may bubble over if baked in too small a dish; if the container is too large, food can dry out. Also keep in mind that food prepared in a deep casserole requires more cooking time than that cooked in a shallower one.

A *baking dish* is shallow and usually square or rectangular. To determine its dimensions, measure across the top from the inside edges. When you need a cover, use foil.

A *casserole* is deeper and often has a fitted cover. To find its volume, fill to the top with water, measuring as you fill.

Herb-seasoned stuffing mix makes a crispy coating for perch fillets in *Fish and Chip Bake.* The fish bakes atop a bed of instant mashed potatoes, chopped spinach, and sour cream.

Fish and Chip Bake

Packaged instant mashed potatoes (enough for 4 servings)
1 **10-ounce package frozen chopped spinach, cooked and well drained**
½ **cup dairy sour cream**
Dash pepper
1 **16-ounce package frozen perch fillets, thawed**
¼ **cup milk**
½ **cup herb-seasoned stuffing mix, crushed**
2 **tablespoons butter *or* margarine, melted**
Lemon slices

Prepare potatoes according to package directions, *except* reduce water by ¼ cup. Stir in drained spinach, sour cream, and pepper. Turn into a 10x6x2-inch baking dish.

Skin fish fillets. Dip one side of each fillet in milk, then in crushed stuffing mix. Fold fillets in half, coating side out. Place atop potato mixture; drizzle with melted butter. Bake, uncovered, at 350° till fish flakes easily when tested with a fork, 30 to 35 minutes. Serve with lemon slices. Makes 4 or 5 servings.

Clam Chowder Pie

2 cups chopped potato
¼ cup chopped onion
2 7½-ounce cans minced clams
2 tablespoons butter
2 tablespoons snipped parsley
4 teaspoons all-purpose flour
¼ teaspoon salt
   Dash pepper
¾ cup milk
   Plain Pastry (see page 12)

Cook potato and onion in 1 cup water till tender; drain. Drain clams, reserving ½ cup liquid. In saucepan melt butter; stir in parsley, flour, salt, and dash pepper. Add reserved clam liquid and milk all at once; cook and stir till thickened and bubbly. Stir in cooked potato mixture and clams. Turn into a 9-inch pie plate.

Prepare Plain Pastry. Roll out to a 10-inch circle; place atop filling. Turn edges under and flute; cut slits for escape of steam. Bake, uncovered, at 425° for 25 to 30 minutes. Let stand 5 minutes before serving. Makes 6 servings.

Shaker Fish Pie

1 pound fresh or frozen fish
   Plain Pastry (see page 12)
1 cup chopped onion
½ cup chopped celery
3 tablespoons butter
1 tablespoon snipped parsley
½ teaspoon dried marjoram,
   crushed
2 tablespoons all-purpose flour
1 teaspoon salt
   Dash pepper
1 cup light cream
⅓ cup fine dry bread crumbs
2 tablespoons butter, melted

Thaw frozen fish. Cook the fish in boiling salted water to cover till fish flakes easily when tested with a fork. Drain; break fish into chunks.

Prepare Plain Pastry for a single-crust pie. Do not prick. Bake pastry shell at 450° for 15 minutes. Remove from oven; set aside. Reduce oven temperature to 325°.

Meanwhile, cook onion and celery in the 3 tablespoons butter till onion is tender. Stir in parsley and marjoram. Blend in flour, salt, and pepper. Add cream; cook and stir till thickened and bubbly. Remove from heat; stir in fish. Turn mixture into partially baked 9-inch pastry shell.

Toss together bread crumbs and melted butter; sprinkle over pie. Bake, uncovered, at 325° for 30 to 35 minutes. Let stand 5 minutes. Makes 6 servings.

Tuna-Noodle Casserole

6 cups water
1 8-ounce package frozen noodles
1 cup chopped celery
¼ cup chopped onion
2 tablespoons butter or
   margarine
2 tablespoons all-purpose flour
1 11-ounce can condensed
   Cheddar cheese soup
¾ cup milk
1 9¼-ounce can tuna, drained
   and flaked
¼ cup chopped pimiento
¼ cup thinly sliced pitted ripe
   olives
¼ cup grated Parmesan cheese

In saucepan bring water to boiling; add frozen noodles, stirring till separated. Boil rapidly till tender, 15 to 20 minutes. Drain and set aside.

Meanwhile, in saucepan cook celery and onion in butter till tender. Blend in flour; stir in cheese soup. Gradually stir in milk. Cook and stir till thickened and bubbly. Stir in tuna, pimiento, olives, and cooked noodles.

Turn into a 2-quart casserole; top with Parmesan. Bake, uncovered, at 375° for 25 minutes. Makes 6 servings.

Microwave cooking directions: On range top cook and drain noodles as directed above. Meanwhile, in a 1½-quart nonmetal casserole cook celery and onion in butter, covered, in a countertop microwave oven till tender, 3½ to 4 minutes, stirring twice. Blend in flour; stir in soup and milk.

Micro-cook, uncovered, till thickened and bubbly, about 4 minutes, stirring after each minute. Fold in tuna, pimiento, and cooked noodles. Micro-cook, uncovered, till heated through, 3 to 4 minutes, stirring after 2 minutes. Stir; sprinkle with olives and Parmesan.

Tuna-Macaroni Casserole

4 ounces small shell macaroni
1 10¾-ounce can condensed
   cream of celery soup
⅓ cup milk
¼ cup mayonnaise *or* salad
   dressing
½ teaspoon dry mustard
1 cup shredded American cheese
1 6½- *or* 7-ounce can tuna,
   drained and flaked
¼ cup chopped pimiento
¼ cup fine dry bread crumbs
1 tablespoon butter, melted
½ teaspoon paprika

Cook macaroni according to package directions; drain. In bowl blend together soup, milk, mayonnaise, and mustard. Stir in cheese, tuna, and pimiento. Gently fold in cooked macaroni. Turn into a 1½-quart casserole.

Combine crumbs, melted butter, and paprika; sprinkle atop casserole. Bake, uncovered, at 350° till heated through, 45 to 50 minutes. Garnish casserole with parsley sprig, if desired. Makes 4 or 5 servings.

Curried Seafood Bake

3½ ounces elbow macaroni (1 cup)
¼ cup sliced green onion
   with tops
½ teaspoon curry powder
3 tablespoons butter
3 tablespoons all-purpose flour
½ teaspoon salt
1¾ cups milk
1 cup dairy sour cream
1 5-ounce can lobster *or* one
   7½-ounce can crab meat,
   drained, flaked, and
   cartilage removed
1 4½-ounce can shrimp, drained
½ cup coarsely crushed rich
   round crackers
1 tablespoon butter, melted

Cook macaroni according to package directions; drain. Cook onion and curry in the 3 tablespoons butter till onion is tender. Stir in flour and salt. Add milk; cook and stir till thickened and bubbly. Remove from heat; stir in sour cream. Stir in macaroni and seafood. Turn into a 2-quart casserole. Mix crumbs and melted butter; sprinkle around edge. Bake, uncovered, at 350° for 30 minutes. Serves 4 to 6.

Microwave cooking directions: On range top cook macaroni according to package directions; drain. In a 2-quart nonmetal casserole cook onion and curry in the 3 tablespoons butter, covered, in a countertop microwave oven till onion is tender, about 2 minutes. Blend in flour and salt; stir in milk. Micro-cook, uncovered, 1½ minutes; stir. Micro-cook, uncovered, 3 minutes more, stirring after every minute. Stir in sour cream; gently stir in macaroni and seafood. Micro-cook, uncovered, till hot, about 7 minutes, stirring twice. Toss crumbs with melted butter; sprinkle atop.

Shrimp and Noodle Bake

4 ounces wide noodles
1 7-ounce package frozen
   shelled shrimp
¼ cup chopped onion
3 tablespoons butter
3 tablespoons all-purpose flour
½ teaspoon salt
½ teaspoon dried dillweed
2 cups milk
⅓ cup grated Parmesan cheese
½ of a 3-ounce can French-fried
   onions

Cook noodles according to package directions; drain and set aside. Cook frozen shrimp according to package directions; drain and set aside.

In saucepan cook chopped onion in butter till tender but not brown. Stir in flour, salt, and dillweed. Add milk all at once; cook and stir till thickened and bubbly. Stir in Parmesan. Gently stir in cooked noodles and shrimp.

Turn mixture into a 1½-quart casserole. Bake, covered, at 350° till heated through, about 30 minutes. Sprinkle French-fried onions around edges of casserole. Bake, uncovered, 5 minutes longer. Garnish with a sprig of dill, if desired. Makes 5 or 6 servings.

Tuna-Macaroni Casserole, Curried Seafood Bake, and *Shrimp and Noodle Bake* go together in a jiffy with pull-from-the-shelf ingredients. These cupboard casseroles are great for busy families.

Macaroni and Cheese

6 ounces elbow macaroni
  (1½ cups)
3 tablespoons butter *or*
  margarine
¼ cup finely chopped onion
  (optional)
2 tablespoons all-purpose flour
½ teaspoon salt
  Dash pepper
2 cups milk
2 cups cubed sharp American
  cheese (8 ounces)
1 medium tomato, sliced
  Salt

Cook macaroni according to package directions; drain. In saucepan melt butter or margarine. If using onion, cook it in butter till tender but not brown. Blend in flour, the ½ teaspoon salt, and pepper. Add milk all at once; cook and stir till thickened and bubbly. Add cubed cheese to sauce; stir till melted.

Stir cheese sauce into macaroni. Turn mixture into a 1½-quart casserole. Sprinkle tomato slices with a little salt; arrange atop macaroni. Bake, uncovered, at 350° till heated through, 30 to 35 minutes. Makes 6 servings.

Classic Cheese Strata

8 slices day-old bread
6 ounces sharp American cheese
  or Swiss cheese, sliced
4 eggs
2½ cups milk
¼ cup finely chopped onion
1½ teaspoons salt
½ teaspoon prepared mustard
  Dash pepper
  Paprika

Trim crusts from *4 slices* of the bread. Cut trimmed slices in half diagonally to make 8 triangles; set aside. Arrange trimmings and remaining 4 slices untrimmed bread to cover bottom of a 9x9x2-inch baking pan.

Place cheese slices over bread in baking pan. Arrange the 8 bread triangles in 2 rows over cheese. (Points should slightly overlap bases of preceding triangles.)

Beat eggs; blend in milk, chopped onion, salt, mustard, and pepper. Pour over bread and cheese layers. Sprinkle with paprika. Cover and let stand 1 hour at room temperature or several hours in the refrigerator.

Bake, uncovered, at 325° till knife inserted off-center comes out clean, about 1 hour. Let stand 5 minutes before serving. Makes 6 servings.

Acapulco Bean Casserole

1 cup chopped celery
½ cup chopped onion
2 tablespoons butter *or*
  margarine
1 15-ounce can chili with beans
1 8¾-ounce can whole kernel
  corn, drained
2 3⅛-ounce cans jalapeño
  bean dip
1 4-ounce can taco sauce
⅛ teaspoon salt
6 corn tortillas, torn
½ cup shredded sharp American
  cheese *or* sharp Cheddar
  cheese (2 ounces)

In saucepan cook celery and onion in butter or margarine till tender, about 10 minutes. Stir in chili with beans, drained corn, bean dip, taco sauce, and salt.

Arrange *half* the torn tortillas in an 8x1½-inch round baking dish; top with *half* the chili mixture. Repeat layers using remaining torn tortillas and chili mixture.

Bake, covered, at 350° for 35 to 40 minutes. Sprinkle with shredded cheese. Bake, uncovered, till cheese melts, 2 to 3 minutes more. Makes 4 servings.

Microwave cooking directions: In glass bowl combine celery, onion, and butter. Cook, covered, in a countertop microwave oven till tender, about 5 minutes, stirring once. Stir in chili, corn, bean dip, taco sauce, and salt. Micro-cook, covered, till hot, 7 to 8 minutes, stirring twice.

Arrange *half* the torn tortillas in an 8x1½-inch round non-metal baking dish; top with *half* the chili mixture. Repeat layers using remaining torn tortillas and chili mixture.

Micro-cook, covered, till hot, about 4 minutes, giving dish a half turn after 2 minutes. Top with cheese.

How to Freeze Casseroles

Your freezer can be a big help to you in planning and preparing meals. First, it allows you to stock up on bargain-priced and in-season foods (freeze a batch of stew when stew meat is on sale, a zucchini casserole when zucchini's at its best). Second, it affords you the flexibility of making casseroles ahead (if you're serving one tonight, fix twice as much as you need and freeze the extra for that busy day when supper is the last thing you want to think about).

To prepare foods for freezing:
• Freeze most casseroles before baking, especially when all the ingredients are already cooked. Exceptions to this are dishes that contain uncooked rice, raw vegetables, or uncooked meat that has been frozen and thawed.
• Do not freeze mixtures containing hard-cooked egg whites, raw vegetables, mayonnaise, or sour cream.
• Undercook starchy ingredients such as beans, rice, and noodles, as they can become mushy when frozen. Potatoes become especially soft.
• Freeze casserole toppings separately to keep them from becoming soggy. Keep a supply of plain or buttered crumbs in the freezer to use on frozen casseroles.
• Do not freeze baked pastry; add fresh or frozen *unbaked* pastry during reheating.
• Season foods lightly before freezing, then add more when reheating. Cloves, pepper, garlic, and celery become stronger on freezing; onion, salt, and chili powder weaken.
• Freeze casseroles either in quantities just right for your family or in individual servings.

To freeze:
• Chill hot casseroles rapidly. Set pan of hot food in ice water; cool to room temperature. Wrap, label, and freeze.
• When possible, use shallow baking dishes to speed freezing and thawing of casseroles.
• Allow some headspace to permit expansion of food.
• Cover casseroles with moisture-vaporproof material such as freezer paper, heavy foil, plastic wrap, or a tight-fitting lid. Fix tape around the edges to make a tight seal. Label contents, number of servings, and date of freezing.
• One handy way to freeze a casserole is to line the dish with heavy foil, leaving a long overhang; prepare casserole as directed. Seal foil over food; freeze. When frozen, remove wrapped casserole from dish. Label and store in the freezer. Reheat in the same casserole dish.

To serve:
• Use frozen casseroles within 2 or 3 months for best quality.
• The size of the frozen casserole affects baking time. Shallow dishes and smaller quantities of food require less reheating time than deeper, larger casseroles.
• To reheat casserole without thawing, bake, uncovered, at 400° till heated through, 1 to 2 hours for most casseroles.
• To thaw casserole before reheating, let it stand overnight in the refrigerator. Then, cook as directed in the recipe, baking an additional 15 to 30 minutes.
• If gravies or sauces separate on freezing, stirring may help return them to their original consistency.

Step-Saving Combinations

Sour Cream-Chili Bake

1 pound ground beef
1 15-ounce can pinto beans, drained
1 10-ounce can hot enchilada sauce
1 8-ounce can tomato sauce
1 cup shredded sharp American cheese (4 ounces)
1 tablespoon instant minced onion
1 6-ounce package corn chips
1 cup dairy sour cream
½ cup shredded sharp American cheese (2 ounces)

In skillet brown ground beef; drain off fat. Stir in drained beans, enchilada sauce, tomato sauce, the 1 cup shredded cheese, and instant minced onion.

Set aside *1 cup* of the corn chips; coarsely crush remaining chips. Stir crushed chips into meat mixture. Turn into a 1½-quart casserole. Bake, covered, at 375° for 30 minutes.

Spoon sour cream atop casserole; sprinkle with the ½ cup cheese. Sprinkle reserved chips around edge of casserole. Bake, uncovered, 2 to 3 minutes. Makes 6 servings.

Enchilada Squares

1 pound ground beef
¼ cup chopped onion
4 eggs
1 8-ounce can tomato sauce
1 5⅓-ounce can evaporated milk (⅔ cup)
1 1½-ounce envelope enchilada sauce mix
⅓ cup sliced pitted ripe olives
2 cups corn chips
1 cup shredded Cheddar cheese (4 ounces)

In skillet cook beef and onion till meat is brown and onion is tender. Drain off fat. Spread meat mixture in a 10x6x2-inch baking dish.

Beat together eggs, tomato sauce, evaporated milk, and enchilada sauce mix; pour over meat. Sprinkle with olives; top with chips. Bake, uncovered, at 350° till set in center, 20 to 25 minutes. Sprinkle with cheese. Bake till cheese melts, 3 to 5 minutes. Makes 6 servings.

Meat and Potato Pie

1 package piecrust mix (for 2-crust pie)
½ cup milk
½ envelope onion soup mix (¼ cup)
Dash pepper
Dash ground allspice
1 pound ground beef
2 tablespoons snipped parsley
1 tablespoon butter *or* margarine, melted
½ teaspoon salt
1 12-ounce package frozen loose-pack hash brown potatoes, thawed (3 cups)
Warmed catsup

Prepare piecrust mix according to package directions; roll out for a 2-crust 9-inch pie. Line a 9-inch pie plate with *half* of the pastry. Set aside.

In bowl combine milk, dry onion soup mix, pepper, and allspice. Add ground beef; mix thoroughly. Lightly pat meat mixture into pastry-lined pie plate.

Combine parsley, melted butter, and salt; add thawed hash brown potatoes, stirring to coat. Spoon potatoes over meat mixture. Adjust top crust; seal and flute edges. Cut slits for escape of steam.

Bake, uncovered, at 350° till crust is golden, about 1 hour. Serve with warmed catsup. Makes 6 servings.

Quick-mix casseroles such as *Sour Cream-Chili Bake* make excellent use of convenience foods. To complete this speedy supper, thaw frozen avocado dip to spoon over a tossed salad.

Beef-Noodle Bake

4 ounces medium noodles (3 cups)
1 pound ground beef
½ cup chopped onion
¼ cup chopped green pepper
1 15-ounce can tomato sauce
½ teaspoon seasoned salt
¼ teaspoon pepper
2 cups cream-style cottage cheese (16 ounces)
1 3-ounce package cream cheese, softened

Cook noodles according to package directions; drain. In skillet cook beef, onion, and green pepper till meat is brown and vegetables are tender; drain off fat. Stir in tomato sauce, seasoned salt, and pepper.

Blend together cottage cheese and cream cheese till fluffy. Spoon the cooked noodles into a greased 10x6x2-inch baking dish. Spread cheese mixture over noodles; pour meat sauce over all. Bake, uncovered, at 350° till heated through, 30 to 40 minutes. Makes 6 servings.

Macaroni and Meatballs

2 beaten eggs
¾ cup soft bread crumbs (1 slice)
2 tablespoons finely chopped onion
2 tablespoons finely chopped green pepper
2 tablespoons snipped parsley
1 teaspoon dried oregano, crushed
¼ teaspoon garlic salt
1 pound ground beef
1 7¼-ounce package macaroni and cheese dinner mix
1 2½-ounce envelope sour cream sauce mix
2 cups milk

In medium bowl combine eggs, bread crumbs, onion, green pepper, parsley, *½ teaspoon* of the oregano, garlic salt, and dash pepper. Add ground beef; mix well. Shape into 24 meatballs. Place in shallow baking pan. Bake, uncovered, at 375° for about 20 minutes.

Meanwhile, cook macaroni from dinner mix in boiling salted water according to package directions; drain. Combine dry cheese mix from packaged dinner, sour cream sauce mix, and the remaining ½ teaspoon oregano; beat in milk. Stir in cooked macaroni.

Turn mixture into a 12x7½x2-inch baking dish. Arrange meatballs atop. Bake, uncovered, at 375° till heated through, 20 to 25 minutes. Makes 6 servings.

Festive Hash and Eggs

1 15-ounce can corned beef hash
4 eggs
½ cup milk
½ cup shredded Swiss cheese
Paprika

Spread hash in 4 individual casseroles. Make a depression in each with back of spoon. Break *one* egg into each; do not season. Spoon *2 tablespoons* milk over each; top with cheese. Bake, uncovered, at 350° till almost set, 18 to 20 minutes. Top with paprika; let stand 5 minutes. Makes 4 servings.

Make Your Own Bread Crumbs

Soft crumbs: Tear slices of fresh bread into quarters. Place a few at a time in blender container; cover and blend till coarsely chopped. Or, tear bread into crumbs. Each slice makes about ¾ cup soft crumbs.
Fine dry crumbs: Oven-toast stale bread at 300° till crisp and dry. Crush with a rolling pin. Or, add to blender container a little at a time; cover and blend till finely crushed. Each slice makes about ¼ cup fine dry crumbs.
Buttered crumbs: Add 1 tablespoon melted butter to ¾ cup soft crumbs *or* ¼ cup fine dry crumbs; toss to combine.

Corned Beef-Macaroni Pie

3½ ounces elbow macaroni (1 cup)
1 beaten egg
1 8-ounce can tomato sauce
¼ cup chopped onion
½ teaspoon prepared mustard
½ teaspoon prepared
    horseradish
1 12-ounce can corned beef,
    finely flaked
¾ cup shredded sharp American
    cheese (3 ounces)
1 beaten egg
½ teaspoon dried basil, crushed
¾ cup soft bread crumbs
    (1 slice)
1 tablespoon butter *or*
    margarine, melted

Cook macaroni in large amount of boiling *unsalted* water till tender, about 10 minutes; drain and set aside.

Meanwhile, combine 1 beaten egg, ¼ *cup* of the tomato sauce, onion, mustard, and horseradish. Add corned beef; mix well. Press mixture into bottom and sides of a 9-inch pie plate, forming a shell; set aside.

Combine cooked macaroni with shredded cheese, the remaining tomato sauce, 1 beaten egg, and basil. Turn mixture into the corned beef shell.

Toss bread crumbs with melted butter or margarine; sprinkle atop macaroni mixture. Bake, uncovered, at 350° till heated through, 25 to 30 minutes. Makes 6 servings.

Frank and Corn Crown

½ cup chopped green pepper
¼ cup chopped onion
2 tablespoons butter *or*
    margarine
2¾ cups soft bread crumbs
    (about 4 slices)
1 17-ounce can cream-style corn
1 12-ounce can whole kernel
    corn, drained
2 beaten eggs
1 teaspoon salt
1 tablespoon butter *or*
    margarine, melted
1 pound frankfurters, halved
    crosswise (8 to 10)

Cook green pepper and onion in the 2 tablespoons butter till tender but not brown. Add *2 cups* of the bread crumbs, cream-style corn, whole kernel corn, eggs, and salt; mix lightly. Spoon mixture into an 8x1½-inch round baking dish.

Combine the remaining ¾ cup bread crumbs and the 1 tablespoon melted butter or margarine; sprinkle atop corn mixture. Bake, uncovered, at 350° for 30 minutes.

Stand franks, cut end down, around edge of baking dish to form crown. Bake, uncovered, till franks are hot and knife inserted in corn mixture comes out clean, 10 to 15 minutes longer. Makes 5 or 6 servings.

Savory Frank-Noodle Bake

1 cup medium noodles
½ cup chopped onion
1 tablespoon butter *or* margarine
3 beaten eggs
1 8-ounce can imitation sour
    cream (1 cup)
½ cup cream-style cottage
    cheese
½ pound frankfurters, thinly
    sliced (4 or 5)
½ teaspoon salt
    Dash pepper
½ cup cornflake crumbs
1 tablespoon butter *or*
    margarine, melted

Cook noodles according to package directions; drain. In small skillet cook onion in the 1 tablespoon butter or margarine till tender but not brown.

Combine eggs, imitation sour cream, cottage cheese, frankfurters, cooked onion, cooked noodles, salt, and pepper. Turn mixture into a 1-quart casserole.

Toss cornflake crumbs with the melted butter or margarine; sprinkle atop casserole. Bake, uncovered, at 350° till heated through, 40 to 45 minutes. Makes 4 servings.

Substantial *Salmon-Macaroni Pie* is an easy put-together that even young cooks can
master. This flavor-packed casserole features salmon, shredded cheese, and canned macaroni.

Salmon-Macaroni Pie

4 beaten eggs
2 15-ounce cans macaroni in
   cheese sauce
1 16-ounce can salmon, drained,
   bones and skin removed,
   and broken into chunks
1½ cups soft bread crumbs (2 slices)
1 cup shredded sharp American
   cheese (4 ounces)
¼ teaspoon salt

In large bowl stir together beaten eggs, macaroni in cheese sauce, salmon chunks, soft bread crumbs, shredded American cheese, and salt.

Turn mixture into a greased 10-inch oven-going skillet or a 10x6x2-inch baking dish. Bake, uncovered, at 350° till set in center, 40 to 45 minutes. Cut in wedges or squares; garnish each serving with a parsley sprig, if desired. Makes 6 to 8 servings.

Fish Florentine

6 frozen breaded fish portions
1 10-ounce package frozen
   chopped spinach
1 10-ounce package frozen Welsh
   rarebit, thawed
1 5-ounce can water chestnuts,
   drained and chopped (½ cup)
6 slices bacon, crisp-cooked,
   drained, and crumbled

Fry fish according to package directions. Meanwhile, cook spinach according to package directions; drain.

In medium saucepan stir together spinach, rarebit, water chestnuts, and bacon; heat through. Spread spinach mixture in a 10x6x2-inch baking dish. Top with fish portions.

Bake, uncovered at 350° till heated through, about 10 minutes. Garnish with lemon slices, if desired. Serves 6.

Tuna Salad Bake (pictured on page 6)

1 package refrigerated crescent
   rolls (8 rolls)
1 9¼-ounce can tuna, drained and
   flaked
½ cup chopped celery
¼ cup green goddess salad
   dressing
2 cups chopped lettuce
2 medium tomatoes, sliced
4 slices American cheese,
   halved diagonally (4 ounces)

Unroll dough and separate into 8 triangles. Place in a greased 9-inch pie plate, pressing edges together to form a pie shell. Bake, uncovered, at 350° for 10 minutes.

Meanwhile, toss tuna and celery with salad dressing; spread mixture over partially baked shell. Sprinkle with chopped lettuce; arrange tomato slices atop. Bake, uncovered, 10 minutes longer. Top with cheese halves; bake 10 minutes more. Makes 6 servings.

Tuna-Rice Soufflé

1 10¾-ounce can condensed
   cream of mushroom soup
1 6½- or 7-ounce can tuna,
   drained and flaked
1 cup cooked rice
¼ cup chopped pimiento
2 tablespoons snipped parsley
4 eggs, separated

In saucepan heat and stir condensed soup. Stir in tuna, cooked rice, pimiento, and parsley; heat through.

Beat egg whites to stiff peaks; set aside. Beat yolks till thick and lemon-colored; slowly stir in tuna mixture. Fold into beaten egg whites; turn into an ungreased 2-quart soufflé dish. Bake, uncovered, at 350° till set in center, 30 to 35 minutes. Serve immediately with a cheese sauce, if desired. Makes 6 servings.

Creamy Chicken Casserole

3½ **ounces elbow macaroni (1 cup)**
¾ **cup milk**
1 **10 ¾-ounce can condensed cream of chicken soup**
2 **cups chopped cooked chicken**
1 **cup shredded sharp American cheese (4 ounces)**
1 **4-ounce can mushroom stems and pieces, drained**
¼ **cup chopped pimiento**

Cook macaroni according to package directions; drain. In a bowl stir milk into soup. Add chicken, *half* the cheese, the mushrooms, pimiento, and cooked macaroni; mix well.

Turn mixture into a 2-quart casserole. Bake, covered, at 350° for 50 minutes. Uncover and stir. Top with the remaining cheese; bake till cheese melts, 2 to 3 minutes longer. Makes 6 servings.

Deep-Dish Chicken Pie

1 **cup packaged biscuit mix**
½ **teaspoon dried sage, crushed**
1 **10½-ounce can chicken gravy**
1 **4-ounce can mushroom stems and pieces, drained**
2 **tablespoons sliced pimiento-stuffed green olives**
  Dash pepper
2 **5-ounce cans boned chicken**

In bowl combine biscuit mix and sage. Prepare biscuit dough according to package directions for biscuits, *except* substitute ¼ *cup* of the chicken gravy for the liquid. Roll out on waxed paper to an 8-inch circle; set aside.

In saucepan combine remaining gravy with mushrooms, olives, and pepper; stir in chicken with its broth. Bring to boiling; turn into an 8x1½-inch round baking dish. Invert dough onto *hot* sauce; remove paper. Bake, uncovered, at 450° till topper is done, 12 to 15 minutes. Makes 6 servings.

Maple-Glazed Meat and Beans

1 **12-ounce can luncheon meat**
¼ **cup maple-flavored syrup**
1 **21-ounce can pork and beans in tomato sauce**
¼ **cup finely chopped onion**
1 **tablespoon all-purpose flour**
1 **teaspoon prepared mustard**
¼ **cup shredded sharp American cheese (1 ounce)**

Cut luncheon meat into 8 slices; brush each slice with some of the syrup, reserving remaining syrup. Arrange meat around edge of a 9-inch pie plate, overlapping slightly.

In saucepan combine beans, the remaining syrup, onion, flour, and mustard. Cook and stir till thickened and bubbly; pour boiling bean mixture into pie plate. Sprinkle with cheese. Bake, uncovered, at 350° till meat is lightly browned, about 20 minutes. Makes 4 servings.

How to Make Croutons

Brush bread slices lightly with oil or melted butter, if desired. Cut into ½-inch cubes. For seasoned croutons, sprinkle with garlic powder or crushed dried herbs.
In the oven: Spread bread cubes in a shallow baking pan. Bake at 300° till dry, 20 to 25 minutes, stirring once.
In the microwave oven: Spread bread cubes in a shallow baking dish. Micro-cook, uncovered, till crisp and dry, about 6 minutes for 4 cups croutons; stir every 2 minutes.
Cheese croutons: Make croutons, using butter or margarine. Sprinkle with grated Parmesan cheese while hot; cool.

You'll save double the time when you make *Pork and Apples with Stuffing* and
freeze half to serve later. For a quick garnish, poach apple slices two minutes in a little water.

Pork and Apples with Stuffing

3 pounds pork tenderloin
2 tablespoons cooking oil
2 20-ounce cans pie-sliced
   apples, drained
½ cup packed brown sugar
6 cups herb-seasoned stuffing
   mix
½ cup chopped celery
¼ cup butter *or* margarine,
   melted
3 tablespoons instant minced
   onion
1 teaspoon salt
½ teaspoon ground sage
2 cups beef broth

Have your meatman cut the pork tenderloin into 12 slices and
flatten each slice. Sprinkle meat slices with a little salt and
pepper. In a skillet brown meat well on both sides in hot
cooking oil. Divide the pork tenderloin slices between two
12x7½x2-inch baking dishes.

Combine apples and brown sugar. Spoon over tenderloin
slices. Combine stuffing mix, celery, melted butter or margarine, onion, salt, and sage; toss with beef broth till moistened.
Press stuffing into ½ cup measure; unmold a stuffing mound
onto each tenderloin slice.

Bake, uncovered, at 375° till pork is done, about 1 hour.
Garnish with parsley and poached fresh apple slices, if desired. Makes 2 casseroles, 6 servings each.

To freeze: Omit baking casseroles; wrap securely, label,
and freeze. Bake frozen casseroles, covered, at 400° till pork
is done, about 1¼ hours.

Sauerkraut and Sausage Bake

1½ pounds bulk pork sausage
 1 27-ounce can sauerkraut,
     rinsed, drained, and snipped
 1 tablespoon sliced green onion
     with tops
     Packaged instant mashed
     potatoes (enough for
     4 servings)
 4 tablespoons grated Parmesan
     cheese

In skillet brown sausage; drain off fat. Stir together sauerkraut and green onion; turn into a 1½-quart casserole. Spoon sausage over sauerkraut mixture.

Prepare mashed potatoes according to package directions. Stir 2 *tablespoons* of the cheese into potatoes. Spread potatoes over sausage; sprinkle with remaining 2 tablespoons cheese. Bake, uncovered, at 400° till heated through, 35 to 40 minutes. Makes 6 servings.

Red-Ribbon Cheese Casserole

 1 7-ounce package macaroni
     (2 cups)
 1 10¾-ounce can condensed
     tomato soup
 1 10¾-ounce can condensed
     cream of chicken soup
 ½ cup milk
 8 slices American cheese
     (8 ounces)
 7 tomato slices
1½ cups soft bread crumbs
     (2 slices)
 2 tablespoons butter *or*
     margarine, melted

Cook macaroni according to package directions; drain. Stir together soups and milk; stir in cooked macaroni.

Turn mixture into a 12x7½x2-inch baking dish. Alternate cheese and tomato slices down center of casserole. Toss crumbs with melted butter; sprinkle atop. Bake, uncovered, at 350° for 30 minutes. Serves 6 to 8.

Triple-Cheese Pie

 1 package piecrust mix
     (for 2-crust pie)
 ¼ cup all-purpose flour
 1 egg yolk
1½ cups dry cottage cheese
     (12 ounces)
 3 eggs
 ⅓ cup grated Parmesan cheese
 ⅛ teaspoon pepper
 1 cup finely chopped fully
     cooked ham
 1 4-ounce can mushroom stems
     and pieces, drained
 1 6-ounce package sliced
     mozzarella cheese

Combine piecrust mix and flour; stir in water according to package directions. Roll out *half* the dough; fit into a 10-inch pie plate. Flute edges. Combine egg yolk and 1 tablespoon water; brush *half* the mixture over pastry shell. Prick lightly with a fork. Roll out remaining pastry dough to an 8½-inch circle. Cut into 6 wedges; place on an ungreased baking sheet. Bake pastry shell and wedges at 450° till lightly browned, 8 to 10 minutes. Remove from oven; reduce oven temperature to 375°.

In mixing bowl beat dry cottage cheese, eggs, Parmesan cheese, and pepper at medium speed of electric mixer till fluffy, 3 to 4 minutes. Stir in ham and mushrooms.

Arrange *half* the mozzarella cheese slices in baked pastry shell; pour *half* the ham mixture over cheese-lined pastry. Repeat layers.

Place pastry wedges atop pie. Brush wedges with remaining egg yolk mixture. Bake, uncovered, at 375° till set, about 35 minutes. (Center will look slightly watery.) Let stand 10 minutes before serving. Makes 6 servings.

Microwave Know-How

Your microwave oven can save you plenty of time when you prepare casseroles, regardless of whether you use the conventional or the microwave oven for the final heating. It's ideal for melting butter or margarine, cooking onion in butter, cooking ground beef or bacon, and preparing sauces.

Use the timings in the chart below to help make meal preparation easy. And read the information at the bottom of the page for help in choosing containers and timing recipes. Then, check the index to find several recipes with complete microwave directions as well as conventional methods.

Step	Amount	Special Directions	Cooking Time
Melt butter	2 tablespoons	Uncovered	30 to 40 seconds
Toast nuts	¼ cup	Use shallow dish; stir frequently	3 minutes
Cook onions in butter or oil	½ cup chopped onion 1 tablespoon butter or cooking oil	Cover; stir once	2 to 3 minutes
Cook ground beef	1 pound	Crumble into bowl; cover; stir several times	5 minutes
Cook bacon	4 slices	Cook between layers of paper toweling in a shallow dish	2½ to 3½ minutes
Make white sauce	2 tablespoons butter 2 tablespoons flour ¼ teaspoon salt 1 cup milk	Melt butter	30 to 40 seconds
		Stir in flour and salt; then stir in milk	1 minute
		Stir every 30 seconds till thickened	2 to 3 minutes

Special Helps

Use heat-resistant glass and glass-ceramic containers—no metals—in the microwave oven. For short-time cooking you can cook on paper or in plastic dishes. To cover casseroles, use a fitted lid, waxed paper, or a dinner plate.

Because so many variables enter into microwave cooking, times given here are only approximate. For this book, recipes were tested with countertop microwave ovens rated at 600 to 700 watts. If yours has a lower wattage, expect to increase the cooking time. For an oven with a higher wattage, shorten the cooking time.

Other factors such as the starting temperature, the shape, and the amount of food in the oven can affect the timing, too, so be sure to watch the food carefully.

Make the Most of Leftovers

Ham-Potato Bake

2 15- or 16-ounce cans sliced
    potatoes, drained, *or* 4 cups
    sliced cooked potatoes
2 medium carrots, shredded
    (1 cup)
1½ cups cubed fully cooked ham
1 10 ¾-ounce can condensed
    cream of mushroom soup
½ cup shredded sharp American
    cheese (2 ounces)
¼ cup milk
1 tablespoon instant minced
    onion
⅛ teaspoon pepper
¾ cup soft bread crumbs
    (1 slice)
½ cup shredded sharp American
    cheese (2 ounces)
1 tablespoon butter *or*
    margarine, melted

Layer *half* the potatoes and *half* the carrots in a 2-quart casserole. Stir together cubed ham, condensed mushroom soup, the ½ cup shredded cheese, milk, instant minced onion, and pepper. Pour *half* the ham mixture over potatoes and carrots in casserole. Repeat layers.

Combine soft bread crumbs, the ½ cup shredded cheese, and melted butter; sprinkle over casserole. Bake, uncovered, at 350° till heated through, about 45 minutes. Garnish with parsley sprigs, if desired. Makes 4 to 6 servings.

Ham and Vegetables Mornay (pictured on the cover)

2¼ pounds potatoes,
    peeled and cut up
    (7 medium)
1 beaten egg *or*
    2 beaten egg yolks
2 tablespoons snipped chives
    or sliced green onion
    with tops
    Paprika
1 10-ounce package frozen mixed
    vegetables *or* 2 cups
    leftover cooked vegetables
3 tablespoons butter *or*
    margarine
3 tablespoons all-purpose
    flour
½ teaspoon salt
⅛ teaspoon white pepper
⅛ teaspoon ground nutmeg
1½ cups milk
½ cup shredded Swiss cheese
    (2 ounces)
1 tablespoon grated Parmesan
    cheese
2 cups cubed fully cooked ham
1 tablespoon butter *or*
    margarine, melted

In saucepan cook potatoes in boiling salted water to cover till tender, 15 to 20 minutes; drain. Mash with potato masher or electric mixer on lowest speed. Stir beaten egg or egg yolks and chives or green onion into potatoes; season to taste with a little salt and pepper. Spread potato mixture on bottom and sides of a 2-quart casserole to form a shell; sprinkle top edges with paprika.

Cook frozen mixed vegetables according to package directions; drain and set aside.

In saucepan melt the 3 tablespoons butter or margarine; blend in flour, salt, white pepper, and nutmeg. Add milk all at once. Cook and stir till thickened and bubbly. Add Swiss and Parmesan cheeses; stir till melted. Stir in cubed ham and cooked vegetables.

Spoon sauce mixture into potato-lined casserole, being sure mixture is below edge of potato shell. Brush exposed surface of potatoes with the melted butter.

Bake, uncovered, at 375° till mixture is heated through and potatoes are lightly browned, 30 to 35 minutes. Makes 6 to 8 servings.

Next time you plan a ham dinner, buy enough extra to prepare *Ham-Potato Bake.* Sprinkled with cheesy bread crumbs, this delicious casserole makes the most of leftover ham and potatoes.

Ham Pot Pie

½ **cup chopped onion**
3 **tablespoons butter *or***
  margarine
⅓ **cup all-purpose flour**
½ **teaspoon dried basil, crushed**
¼ **teaspoon salt**
2¼ **cups milk**
2 **to 3 cups cubed fully cooked**
  ham
1½ **to 2 cups cooked *or* canned**
  cut green beans
1½ **to 2 cups cooked *or* canned**
  whole kernel corn
2 **tablespoons snipped parsley**
  Plain Pastry (see page 12)

In saucepan cook onion in butter or margarine till tender but not brown. Stir in flour, basil, and salt. Add milk all at once; cook and stir till thickened and bubbly.

Add ham, green beans, corn, and parsley to sauce; mix well. Turn mixture into a 12x7½x2-inch baking dish. Bake, uncovered, at 350° till hot, 35 to 40 minutes.

Meanwhile, prepare Plain Pastry. Roll out ¼ inch thick. Cut into wedges or other shapes. Place cutouts on baking sheet; prick well with a fork. Place baking sheet in oven with casserole the last 20 to 25 minutes. Bake till pastry is golden brown. Arrange the baked pastry cutouts atop casserole. Makes 6 servings.

Stuffed Pepper Cups

1 **10½-ounce can condensed**
  beef broth
1 **soup can water (1¼ cups)**
1 **cup regular rice**
½ **teaspoon salt**
6 **large green peppers**
½ **cup finely chopped onion**
¼ **cup chopped celery**
2 **tablespoons butter *or***
  margarine
1½ **cups chopped fully cooked ham**
¾ **cup soft bread crumbs**
  (1 slice)
1 **tablespoon butter *or***
  margarine, melted

In saucepan bring first 4 ingredients to boiling; stir. Cover; cook slowly till rice is done, 15 to 20 minutes.

Cut tops from peppers; discard seeds and membranes. Chop tops; set aside. Cook peppers in boiling salted water for 5 minutes; drain. Arrange in a 12x7½x2-inch baking dish.

Cook onion, celery, and chopped pepper in the 2 tablespoons butter; stir in ham. Toss with rice; spoon into peppers. Mix crumbs and the melted butter; sprinkle atop peppers. Bake, uncovered, at 350° for 20 to 25 minutes. Serves 6.

Microwave cooking directions: On range top cook first 4 ingredients as directed above.

Cut tops from peppers; discard seeds and membranes. Chop tops; set aside. Place peppers in a 12x7½x2-inch non-metal baking dish; sprinkle insides with salt. Cook, covered, in a countertop microwave oven till nearly tender, about 7 minutes, giving dish a half turn after 4 minutes.

In glass bowl micro-cook onion, celery, and the chopped pepper, covered, in the 2 tablespoons butter for 2 to 3 minutes. Stir in ham; toss with rice. Spoon into peppers. Combine crumbs and the melted butter; sprinkle atop peppers. Micro-cook, uncovered, for 8 to 10 minutes, giving dish a half turn after 4 minutes.

Fruit and Vegetable Garnishes

The most colorful garnish you'll find for a casserole may be an ingredient in the dish itself. Save a few cooked carrot or olive slices, mushrooms, or snipped parsley to sprinkle over the casserole just before serving. Or, slice an extra tomato or green pepper to arrange atop the dish during the last few minutes of baking.

Slices of lemon or avocado perk up a seafood casserole, while pineapple or poached apple slices complement ham and pork dishes. Use your imagination and the available produce to create casseroles that look as good as they taste.

Cranberry-Pork Bake

1 8-ounce can whole cranberry
  sauce
2 tablespoons light corn
  syrup
1 17-ounce can sweet potatoes,
  drained
2 tablespoons butter *or*
  margarine, melted
1 tablespoon brown sugar
1 teaspoon salt
¼ teaspoon ground ginger
2 cups coarsely chopped cooked
  pork

Stir together cranberry sauce and corn syrup; set aside. In mixing bowl beat together sweet potatoes, melted butter, brown sugar, salt, and ginger with electric mixer till well blended. Stir in chopped pork.

Turn sweet potato mixture into a 1-quart casserole. Bake, uncovered, at 350° for 35 minutes. Spread cranberry sauce mixture over top; return to oven till heated through, 5 to 10 minutes longer. Makes 4 servings.

Pork Florentine

2 10-ounce packages frozen
  chopped spinach
1 10¾-ounce can condensed
  cream of chicken soup
¼ cup shredded Swiss cheese
  (1 ounce)
2 tablespoons mayonnaise
  or salad dressing
1 teaspoon lemon juice
½ teaspoon Worcestershire
  sauce
1½ cups chopped cooked pork
1½ cups soft bread crumbs
  (2 slices)
2 tablespoons butter *or*
  margarine, melted

Cook spinach according to package directions, *except* use unsalted water; drain. In saucepan stir together condensed soup, Swiss cheese, mayonnaise, lemon juice, and Worcestershire sauce; bring to boiling. Stir ¾ *cup* of the soup mixture into drained spinach.

Pat spinach mixture into 6 individual casseroles. Sprinkle chopped pork over spinach in casseroles. Spoon remaining soup mixture over all.

Toss together bread crumbs and melted butter or margarine; sprinkle atop casseroles. Bake, uncovered, at 350° till heated through, about 25 minutes. Makes 6 servings.

Apple and Pork Casserole

¼ cup chopped onion
1 tablespoon shortening
1 10½-ounce can chicken
  gravy
3 tablespoons brown sugar
¼ teaspoon ground cinnamon
3 cups cubed cooked pork
2 tart apples, peeled
  and chopped
  Packaged instant mashed
  potatoes (enough for
  4 servings)
¼ cup milk
  Dash pepper
1 beaten egg
½ cup shredded American
  cheese (2 ounces)

In saucepan cook onion in shortening till tender. Stir in gravy, sugar, and cinnamon. Add pork and apples; mix well. Spoon mixture into a 8x1½-inch round baking dish.

Prepare potatoes according to package directions, *except* use ¼ cup milk and dash pepper. Blend egg into potatoes. Spoon potatoes in 6 mounds atop pork mixture.

Bake, uncovered, at 350° for 25 minutes. Sprinkle with shredded cheese; return to oven till cheese melts, about 5 minutes longer. Makes 6 servings.

The family won't mind eating last night's roast beef when you prepare spicy *Beef-Macaroni Italiano.* This popular casserole will find its way into your meal plans frequently.

Beef-Macaroni Italiano

¾ **cup elbow macaroni**
1 **tablespoon butter** *or* **margarine**
2 **tablespoons all-purpose flour**
1 **16-ounce can stewed tomatoes, cut up**
1 **8-ounce can tomato sauce**
¼ **cup dry red wine**
½ **envelope onion soup mix (¼ cup)**
½ **teaspoon dried oregano, crushed**
¼ **teaspoon salt**
  Dash pepper
2 **cups cubed cooked beef**
½ **cup shredded mozzarella cheese (2 ounces)**
  Green pepper rings

Cook macaroni according to package directions; drain. In saucepan melt butter; blend in flour. Stir in undrained stewed tomatoes, tomato sauce, red wine, onion soup mix, oregano, salt, and pepper. Cook and stir till thickened and bubbly. Stir in cubed beef and cooked macaroni.

Spoon mixture into a 1½-quart casserole. Bake, uncovered, at 350° for 20 minutes. Sprinkle with cheese; top with green pepper rings. Return to oven till cheese melts, about 5 minutes more. Makes 4 or 5 servings.

Beefy Onion Pie

2 recipes Plain Pastry
   (see page 12)
1½ cups thinly sliced onion
   (3 medium)
¼ cup chopped green pepper
¼ cup butter *or* margarine
2 cups chopped cooked beef
1 cup dairy sour cream
2 tablespoons all-purpose flour
¾ teaspoon salt
⅛ teaspoon pepper
1 beaten egg
2 tablespoons snipped parsley
2 tablespoons chopped pimiento

Prepare Plain Pastry for a double-crust pie. Set aside. In skillet cook onion and green pepper in butter till tender. Stir in beef; remove from heat. Combine sour cream, flour, salt, and pepper; blend in egg, parsley, and pimiento. Stir into onion-beef mixture; mix well.

Turn beef mixture into pastry-lined 9-inch pie plate. Adjust top crust. Seal and flute edges; cut slits for escape of steam. Bake, uncovered, at 375° till crust is golden, about 40 minutes. Makes 6 servings.

Oven Beef Hash

2 cups finely chopped
   cooked potato
1 13-ounce can evaporated milk
1½ cups finely chopped
   cooked beef
1¼ cups finely crushed rich
   round crackers
   (about 30 crackers)
½ cup shredded carrot
⅓ cup finely chopped onion
⅓ cup snipped parsley
1 tablespoon Worcestershire
   sauce
¾ teaspoon salt
⅛ teaspoon pepper
⅛ teaspoon dried oregano,
   crushed
1 tablespoon butter *or*
   margarine, melted

Lightly stir together potato, evaporated milk, beef, *1 cup* of the crushed crackers, carrot, onion, parsley, Worcestershire sauce, salt, pepper, and oregano. Turn mixture into a 1½-quart casserole.

Combine remaining ¼ cup cracker crumbs and melted butter; sprinkle atop casserole. Bake, covered, at 350° till heated through, 35 to 40 minutes. Makes 4 to 6 servings.

Mexican-Style Hash

2 cups chopped cooked beef
⅓ cup chopped onion
2 tablespoons shortening
1½ cups finely chopped raw
   potato
1 12-ounce can whole kernel
   corn, drained
1 10¾-ounce can condensed
   tomato soup
1½ teaspoons chili powder

In 10-inch oven-going skillet cook beef and onion in shortening till onion is tender, about 5 minutes. Sprinkle with salt and pepper. Add potato, corn, soup, and chili powder; stir to combine. Bake, covered, at 350° for 35 to 40 minutes. Makes 4 servings.

Chicken Puff Casserole

¼ cup butter *or* margarine
¼ cup all-purpose flour
½ teaspoon salt
　Dash pepper
1½ cups milk
1 cup chicken broth
2 cups cubed cooked chicken
　or turkey
1 cup frozen peas, cooked and
　drained
2 tablespoons chopped
　pimiento
3 egg whites
3 egg yolks
½ cup all-purpose flour
1 teaspoon baking powder
½ teaspoon salt
½ teaspoon paprika
½ cup milk
1 tablespoon cooking oil

In saucepan melt butter or margarine; blend in the ¼ cup flour, the ½ teaspoon salt, and pepper. Add the 1½ cups milk and chicken broth all at once. Cook and stir till thickened and bubbly. Stir in chicken or turkey, peas, and pimiento; heat through. Cover and keep hot.

Beat egg whites till stiff peaks form, about 1½ minutes on medium speed of electric mixer; set aside. In small bowl beat egg yolks till thick and lemon-colored, about 5 minutes on high speed of electric mixer.

Stir together the ½ cup flour, baking powder, the ½ teaspoon salt, and paprika. Combine the ½ cup milk and cooking oil. Stir flour mixture into beaten yolks alternately with milk mixture. Fold in beaten egg whites.

Turn hot chicken mixture into an 11x7½x1½-inch baking pan. Spread batter over all. Bake, uncovered, at 425° for 20 to 25 minutes. Makes 4 or 5 servings.

Turkey Soufflé

3 tablespoons butter *or*
　margarine
3 tablespoons all-purpose
　flour
1 teaspoon salt
¼ teaspoon paprika
　Dash pepper
1 cup milk
1 cup finely chopped
　cooked turkey
　or chicken
1 tablespoon snipped
　parsley
1 teaspoon grated onion
3 egg yolks
3 stiffly beaten
　egg whites
1 tablespoon chopped
　onion
1 tablespoon butter *or*
　margarine
1 tablespoon all-purpose
　flour
⅛ teaspoon dried dillweed
⅛ teaspoon salt
　Dash pepper
⅔ cup milk
1 2-ounce can mushroom
　stems and pieces,
　drained

In saucepan melt the 3 tablespoons butter or margarine. Stir in the 3 tablespoons flour, the 1 teaspoon salt, paprika, and the dash pepper. Add 1 cup milk all at once; cook and stir till mixture is thickened and bubbly.

Remove from heat. Stir in finely chopped turkey or chicken, snipped parsley, and grated onion. Set aside.

Beat egg yolks till thick and lemon-colored, about 5 minutes on high speed of electric mixer; slowly add turkey mixture to beaten egg yolks, stirring constantly. Cool mixture slightly, about 5 minutes.

Gradually add turkey mixture to stiffly beaten egg whites, folding together thoroughly. Turn into an ungreased 1-quart soufflé dish. Bake, uncovered, at 325° till knife inserted off-center comes out clean, about 50 minutes.

Meanwhile, prepare mushroom-dill sauce. In small saucepan cook chopped onion in the 1 tablespoon butter or margarine till onion is tender but not brown.

Stir the 1 tablespoon flour, dillweed, the ⅛ teaspoon salt, and the dash pepper into cooked onion. Add the ⅔ cup milk all at once; stir in mushroom stems and pieces. Cook and stir till thickened and bubbly. Keep warm till serving time.

When soufflé is done, serve immediately with mushroom-dill sauce. Makes 4 servings.

Curried Turkey Pie

¼ cup light raisins
   Boiling water
1½ cups herb-seasoned
   stuffing mix
¼ cup butter *or* margarine,
   melted
2 tablespoons water
½ cup milk
1 10¾-ounce can condensed
   cream of celery soup
1½ cups cubed cooked turkey
   or chicken
1 cup cooked *or* canned peas
1 2-ounce can chopped
   mushrooms, drained
1 tablespoon finely chopped
   onion
1 to 2 teaspoons curry powder

In small bowl cover raisins with boiling water. Let stand 5 minutes; drain and set aside.

Combine herb-seasoned stuffing mix, melted butter or margarine, and the 2 tablespoons water. Reserving ⅓ cup of the mixture, press remaining stuffing mixture into a 9-inch pie plate to form a pie "shell".

Blend milk into soup; stir in turkey or chicken, peas, mushrooms, onion, curry powder, and drained raisins. Turn mixture into stuffing-lined pie plate.

Sprinkle reserved stuffing mixture over pie. Bake, uncovered, at 375° till pie is heated through, 30 to 35 minutes. Makes 6 servings.

Turkey-Broccoli Bake

2 10-ounce packages frozen
   chopped broccoli
1 tablespoon lemon juice
2 tablespoons butter *or*
   margarine
2 tablespoons all-purpose flour
½ teaspoon salt
2 cups milk
½ cup shredded Swiss cheese
   (2 ounces)
2 cups cooked turkey cut in
   strips
¾ cup soft bread crumbs (1 slice)
¼ cup grated Parmesan cheese
1 tablespoon butter *or*
   margarine, melted

Cook broccoli according to package directions; drain thoroughly. Place broccoli in an 8x1½-inch round baking dish. Sprinkle with lemon juice.

In saucepan melt the 2 tablespoons butter or margarine. Blend in flour and salt. Add milk all at once. Cook and stir till thickened and bubbly. Remove from heat; stir in Swiss cheese till melted. Stir in turkey strips.

Spoon turkey mixture over broccoli in baking dish. Combine bread crumbs, Parmesan, and the melted butter or margarine. Sprinkle over casserole. Bake, uncovered, at 350° till hot, 20 to 25 minutes. Makes 6 servings.

Pastry and Biscuit Tips

For best results every time, keep these tips in mind when topping a casserole with pastry or biscuits:

● Quarter refrigerated biscuits, or cut your favorite biscuit dough (with cheese or herbs, if you like) into 1½-inch rounds to make a mini-biscuit topper.

● To prevent a doughy topper, be sure the casserole mixture is bubbling hot when you add the pastry or biscuit dough.

● Bake pastry cutouts separately, if desired. Place cutouts on a baking sheet; prick with a fork. Bake at 450° till brown, about 12 minutes (time depends on dough's thickness). Arrange atop casserole just before serving.

● To ensure a golden brown color, brush pastry or biscuit dough with a little milk before baking.

Create a Casserole

Contemporary Strata

5 cups cubed day-old bread*
   (about 7 slices)
2 cups finely chopped *or* ground
   cooked meat**
¼ cup chopped green pepper
2 tablespoons very finely
   chopped onion
4 eggs
1 10 ¾-ounce can
   condensed soup***
1 soup can milk (1¼ cups)
½ cup mayonnaise
   Seasoning (optional)****
   Dash cayenne
2 tablespoons butter, melted

Place *2 cups* of the bread cubes in an 8x8x2-inch baking dish. Combine meat, green pepper, and onion; sprinkle over bread in dish. Top with another *2 cups* bread cubes.

Beat eggs; combine with soup, milk, mayonnaise, seasoning, and cayenne. Pour evenly over ingredients in baking dish. Cover and chill for 1 to 3 hours.

Toss remaining 1 cup bread cubes with melted butter; sprinkle atop. Bake, uncovered, at 325° till knife inserted just off-center comes out clean, 50 to 60 minutes. Let stand 5 minutes before serving. Sprinkle with snipped parsley, if desired. Makes 6 servings.

*Bread Suggestions	**Meat Suggestions	***Soup Suggestions	****Seasoning Suggestions
white bread	beef	cream of celery	¼ teaspoon dried thyme, crushed (with beef)
whole wheat bread	pork	cream of mushroom	¼ teaspoon caraway seed (with ham)
rye bread	ham	cream of chicken	½ teaspoon dried sage, crushed (with chicken or turkey)
	chicken or turkey	Cheddar cheese	
	tuna (9¼-ounce can)		

Individual Pot Pies

½ cup chopped celery
½ cup chopped onion
¼ cup chopped green pepper
3 tablespoons butter *or*
   margarine
½ cup all-purpose flour
¼ teaspoon salt
   Seasoning*
⅛ teaspoon pepper
3 cups broth**
2½ cups chopped cooked meat***
1 cup cooked vegetables****
¼ cup chopped pimiento
2 recipes Plain Pastry (see
   page 12)
   Milk

Cook celery, onion, and green pepper in butter till tender. Blend in flour, salt, seasoning, and pepper. Stir in broth all at once; cook and stir till thickened and bubbly. Stir in meat, vegetables, and pimiento. Divide mixture into eight 4¼x1-inch round pie pans (about ¾ cup each).

Prepare Plain Pastry; divide into 8 equal parts. On floured surface roll each part into a 5-inch circle. Place one circle atop each pie; seal to edge of pan. Cut slits in top for escape of steam. Brush with a little milk. Bake, uncovered, at 425° till golden, 25 to 30 minutes. Cover edges with foil last few minutes of baking, if needed, to prevent overbrowning. Makes 8 servings.

To freeze: Do not cut slits or brush with milk until ready to bake. Wrap, label, and freeze unbaked pies. Bake frozen pies at 425° for 45 minutes. *Or,* thaw in refrigerator 5 hours; bake at 425° for 35 minutes.

*Seasoning Suggestions	**Broth Suggestions	***Meat Suggestions	****Vegetable Suggestions
¼ teaspoon dried rosemary, crushed (with beef, pork, or ham)	chicken broth	beef	peas
¼ teaspoon dried dillweed (with chicken, turkey, or tuna)	turkey broth	pork	green beans
	beef broth	ham	sliced carrots
		chicken or turkey	corn
		tuna (two 7-ounce cans)	mixed vegetables

Biscuit-Topped Stew (pictured on page 6)

1 cup packaged biscuit mix
   Biscuit variation (optional)*
¼ cup milk
¼ cup chopped onion
¼ cup chopped green pepper
1 clove garlic, minced
2 tablespoons cooking oil
2 tablespoons all-purpose flour
1 teaspoon sugar
¾ teaspoon salt
   Seasoning (optional)**
⅛ teaspoon pepper
1 16-ounce can tomatoes, cut up
2 cups cubed cooked meat***
1½ to 2 cups cooked vegetables****
1 teaspoon instant chicken or
   beef bouillon granules
1 teaspoon Worcestershire sauce

Stir together biscuit mix and biscuit variation, if desired. Add milk; stir till well blended. On floured surface roll dough to a 5-inch circle. Cut into 6 wedges; set aside.

In saucepan cook onion, green pepper, and garlic in hot oil till onion is tender but not brown. Stir in flour, sugar, salt, seasoning, and pepper. Blend in undrained tomatoes, meat, vegetables, bouillon granules, and Worcestershire sauce. Cook and stir till thickened and bubbly. Turn boiling meat mixture into a 1½-quart casserole. Immediately top with biscuit wedges. Bake, uncovered, at 400° till biscuits are golden, 18 to 20 minutes. Makes 4 to 6 servings.

*Biscuit Variations	**Seasoning Suggestions	***Meat Suggestions	****Vegetable Suggestions
¼ teaspoon dry mustard ½ cup shredded Swiss cheese ½ cup shredded American cheese	¼ teaspoon dried basil, crushed (with beef, pork, or lamb) ¼ teaspoon dried sage, crushed (with chicken or turkey)	beef pork lamb chicken or turkey sliced frankfurters	green beans corn peas mixed vegetables

Meat and Rice Bake

1 10¾-ounce can
   condensed soup*
½ cup dairy sour cream
½ cup milk
1½ cups chopped cooked meat**
1½ cups cooked rice
1 cup cooked or canned peas
1 2-ounce can chopped
   mushrooms, drained
   Seasoning (optional)***
   Crumbs****
1 tablespoon butter, melted

In bowl stir together soup, sour cream, and milk till smooth. Stir in meat, rice, peas, mushrooms, and seasoning. Turn mixture into a 1½-quart casserole. Combine crumbs and melted butter; sprinkle over casserole. Bake, uncovered, at 350° till heated through, 55 to 60 minutes. Makes 4 to 6 servings.

Microwave cooking directions: Prepare casserole as directed above, except do not sprinkle with crumbs. Cook, covered, in a countertop microwave oven till heated through, about 12 minutes, stirring once. Stir again before serving; sprinkle with buttered crumbs.

*Soup Suggestions	**Meat Suggestions	***Seasoning Suggestions	****Crumb Suggestions
cream of mushroom cream of celery Cheddar cheese cream of chicken	beef pork ham chicken or turkey cooked ground beef	1 tablespoon snipped parsley (with any meat) ¼ to ½ teaspoon chili powder (with beef or ground beef) ¼ teaspoon caraway seed (with pork or ham)	¾ cup soft bread crumbs (1 slice) ½ cup crushed crackers (14 crackers) ½ cup crushed pretzels (omit butter)

2 For One or Two Servings

Casseroles tailored to a single serving or twin portions hold the spotlight in this chapter. Most of these tasty mini-meals are so satisfying that there's no need for side dishes, and they're small enough to cook in a tabletop or "toaster" oven rather than heating up the range oven. Several of the recipes even include directions for microwave ovens.

Good things do come in small packages. And *Frank-Stuffed Tomatoes* and *Beef-Stuffed Acorn Squash* are among the best. Both feature a tasty meat mixture tucked inside edible shells.

Baked Eggs and Ham

¼ **cup plain croutons**
2 **teaspoons butter, melted**
1 *or* 2 **eggs**
  Dash pepper
1 **tablespoon shredded cheese**
2 **tablespoons fully cooked**
  ham strips

Toss croutons with melted butter; set aside. Break eggs into a buttered individual casserole. Sprinkle with pepper. Top with cheese; arrange ham atop. Place buttered croutons around edge of dish.

Bake, uncovered, at 350° till eggs are done, 15 to 18 minutes. Makes 1 serving.

Beef-Stuffed Acorn Squash

1 **medium acorn squash**
  (1 pound)
½ **pound ground beef**
2 **tablespoons chopped onion**
2 **tablespoons chopped celery**
2 **tablespoons all-purpose flour**
¼ **teaspoon salt**
¼ **teaspoon ground sage**
¾ **cup milk**
½ **cup cooked rice**
¼ **cup shredded sharp American**
  cheese (1 ounce)

Cut squash in half; discard seeds. Sprinkle squash with a little salt. Bake, cut side down, in 10x6x2-inch baking dish at 350° till tender, 45 to 50 minutes. Cook beef, onion, and celery till meat is brown. Drain off fat. Stir in flour, salt, and sage. Add milk. Cook and stir till thickened and bubbly. Stir in rice. Turn squash cut side up in dish; fill. Bake, uncovered, at 350° for 30 minutes. Top with cheese; bake 3 minutes. Makes 2 servings.

Microwave cooking directions: Pierce whole squash with a cooking fork several times. Place on paper toweling. Cook in a countertop microwave oven till tender, 7 to 8 minutes; turn after 4 minutes. Set aside.

Crumble meat in a 1-quart glass casserole; add onion and celery. Micro-cook, covered, till vegetables are tender, 4 minutes, stirring twice. Drain off fat. Stir in flour, salt, and sage. Add milk; micro-cook, uncovered, till bubbly, 2 to 3 minutes, stirring every 30 seconds. Stir in rice.

Halve squash; discard seeds. Fill squash halves with meat mixture. Place in a 10x6x2-inch glass baking dish or individual bakers. Micro-cook, uncovered, till hot, about 4 minutes. Top with cheese; micro-cook 30 seconds longer.

Frank-Stuffed Tomatoes

2 **large tomatoes**
2 **tablespoons chopped onion**
2 **tablespoons chopped celery**
1 **tablespoon butter** *or*
  margarine
1 **tablespoon all-purpose flour**
⅛ **teaspoon salt**
½ **cup milk**
½ **cup shredded sharp American**
  cheese (2 ounces)
2 **frankfurters** *or* **fully cooked**
  smoked sausage links,
  sliced
½ **cup plain croutons**

Cut tops off tomatoes; scoop out pulp and reserve for another use. Invert tomatoes on paper toweling to drain.

In saucepan cook onion and celery in butter till tender but not brown. Stir in flour and salt. Add milk all at once; cook and stir till thickened and bubbly. Add cheese and franks; cook and stir till cheese melts. Stir in croutons.

Spoon into tomato shells; place in small baking dish. Bake, uncovered, at 350° for 30 minutes. Serves 2.

Microwave cooking directions: Prepare tomatoes as above. In a small glass bowl cook onion and celery in butter, covered, in a countertop microwave oven till tender, about 1½ minutes. Stir in flour and salt. Add milk; micro-cook, uncovered, till thickened and bubbly, about 1½ minutes, stirring every 30 seconds. Stir in cheese and frankfurters. Micro-cook, uncovered, till cheese melts, about 1 minute, stirring after 30 seconds. Stir in croutons.

Spoon mixture into tomato shells. Place in small glass baking dish or 2 individual casseroles. Micro-cook till mixture bubbles and tomatoes are cooked, about 2 minutes.

A cottage cheese filling sparked by chopped chili peppers is the star attraction
in *Chili Manicotti.* Three or four of the large pasta shells will make two generous servings.

Oven Stew for Two

1 tablespoon all-purpose
   flour
¾ teaspoon salt
   Dash pepper
¾ pound boneless beef chuck,
   cut in 1-inch cubes
1 tablespoon shortening
1 10¾-ounce can condensed
   tomato soup
1 soup can water (1¼ cups)
¾ cup chopped onion
¼ teaspoon dried basil, crushed
2 medium potatoes, peeled and
   cubed (2 cups)
2 medium carrots, cut in 1-inch
   pieces (1 cup)
¼ cup dry red wine *or* water

Combine flour, salt, and pepper; coat meat cubes with the seasoned flour. In a small Dutch oven brown meat in hot shortening. Add tomato soup, the soup can of water, chopped onion, and basil.

Bake, covered, at 375° for 1 hour. Add potatoes, carrots, and wine; cover and bake till meat and vegetables are tender, about 1 hour longer. Makes 2 servings.

Chili Manicotti

2 tablespoons chopped onion
1 small clove garlic, minced
1 tablespoon cooking oil
1 11¼-ounce can condensed
   chili beef soup
3 or 4 manicotti shells
1 beaten egg
¾ cup cream-style cottage
   cheese, drained
½ cup shredded sharp American
   cheese (2 ounces)
2 tablespoons chopped canned
   green chili peppers

Cook onion and garlic in oil till tender; stir in soup. Cook manicotti in boiling salted water till tender, 15 to 20 minutes. Drain. Cut shells in half crosswise, if necessary, to fit two individual baking dishes or a 6½x6½x2-inch baking dish.

Combine egg, cottage cheese, *half* the American cheese, and chili peppers. Spoon cheese mixture into manicotti. Pour *half* the soup mixture into the two individual baking dishes or the 6½x6½x2-inch baking dish. Top with stuffed manicotti. Pour remaining soup mixture over, being sure manicotti are coated. Bake, covered, at 350° for 35 to 40 minutes. Uncover; sprinkle with remaining cheese. Bake 2 or 3 minutes more. Let stand 5 minutes. Makes 2 servings.

Macaroni and Cheese for Two

½ cup elbow macaroni
2 tablespoons chopped onion
1 tablespoon butter *or* margarine
4 teaspoons all-purpose flour
1 cup milk
½ teaspoon Worcestershire sauce
¾ cup shredded Cheddar *or*
   American cheese (3 ounces)
¼ cup crushed rich round
   crackers (6 crackers)
1 tablespoon butter, melted

Cook macaroni according to package directions. Drain; set aside. In saucepan cook onion in the 1 tablespoon butter till tender but not brown. Blend in flour. Add milk and Worcestershire sauce all at once; cook and stir till thickened and bubbly. Stir in cheese till melted. Stir in cooked macaroni. Turn mixture into two 10-ounce casseroles.

Combine crushed crackers and the 1 tablespoon melted butter; sprinkle atop casseroles. Bake, uncovered, at 350° for 20 to 25 minutes. Makes 2 servings.

Meatball Meal-in-One

⅓ cup soft bread crumbs
   (½ slice)
2 tablespoons milk
⅛ teaspoon salt
   Dash garlic salt
   Dash dried basil, crushed
¼ pound ground beef
1 small potato, peeled and sliced
1 medium carrot, sliced (½ cup)
1 tablespoon butter *or* margarine
1 tablespoon all-purpose flour
⅛ teaspoon salt
   Dash pepper
½ cup milk
   Paprika

Combine first 5 ingredients. Add meat; mix well. Shape into 4 meatballs; set aside. Combine potato and carrot in a 2½-cup casserole; sprinkle with salt and pepper.

In saucepan melt butter. Stir in flour, the ⅛ teaspoon salt, and the dash pepper. Add the ½ cup milk; cook and stir till thickened and bubbly. Pour over vegetables; top with meatballs. Bake, covered, at 350° for 30 minutes. Uncover; bake 10 minutes longer. Sprinkle with paprika. Makes 1 serving.

Microwave cooking directions: Prepare meatballs as above; place in a 2½-cup glass casserole. Cook, covered, in a countertop microwave oven 3 minutes; remove meatballs. Wipe out dish. In same dish combine potato, carrot, and ¼ cup water. Season with salt and pepper. Micro-cook, covered, 5 minutes. Drain off liquid.

In 1-cup glass measure micro-melt butter 30 to 40 seconds. Stir in flour, the ⅛ teaspoon salt, and the dash pepper. Add the ½ cup milk. Micro-cook, uncovered, 1½ minutes, stirring every 30 seconds. Pour over vegetables; top with meatballs. Micro-cook, covered, 2 minutes. Sprinkle with paprika.

Enchiladas Dos

½ **pound ground beef**
¼ **cup chopped onion**
½ **teaspoon salt**
4 **6-inch flour tortillas**
1 **4-ounce can taco sauce**
½ **cup shredded Cheddar cheese**
2 **tablespoons butter**
2 **tablespoons all-purpose flour**
1 **teaspoon instant chicken**
   bouillon granules
⅔ **cup water**
2 **tablespoons chopped canned**
   green chili peppers
⅓ **cup dairy sour cream**

Cook beef and onion till meat is browned and onion is tender; drain off excess fat. Stir in salt. Divide meat onto tortillas; top *each* with about ¼ of the taco sauce and 1 tablespoon of the cheese. Roll up. Place seam side down in a 10x6x2-inch baking dish.

In saucepan melt butter. Blend in flour and chicken bouillon granules. Stir in water. Cook and stir till thickened and bubbly. Stir in chili peppers. Gradually stir about half the hot mixture into sour cream; return to remaining hot mixture in saucepan. Pour over tortillas in baking dish.

Bake, uncovered, at 350° till heated through, about 15 minutes. Sprinkle with remaining cheese. Bake till cheese melts, about 2 minutes longer. Makes 2 servings.

Shrimp Rockefeller

2 **tablespoons butter** *or*
   margarine
½ **teaspoon celery seed**
½ **teaspoon Worcestershire sauce**
¼ **teaspoon salt**
2 **tablespoons sliced green**
   onion with tops
1 **small clove garlic, minced**
1 **10-ounce package frozen**
   chopped spinach, thawed
½ **cup chopped lettuce**
½ **cup light cream**
1 **beaten egg**
4 **ounces fresh** *or* **frozen**
   shelled shrimp, cooked
2 **tablespoons fine dry bread**
   crumbs
2 **tablespoons grated Parmesan**
   cheese
1 **tablespoon butter, melted**

In medium saucepan combine the 2 tablespoons butter, celery seed, Worcestershire, and salt. Stir in the green onion and garlic. Cook, covered, 2 to 3 minutes. Drain the spinach thoroughly; stir into mixture in saucepan with lettuce, cream, and beaten egg. Cook and stir till mixture just begins to bubble.

Divide *half* the shrimp between two 8-ounce individual casseroles or baking shells. Divide hot spinach mixture between the casseroles; top with remaining shrimp.

Combine the bread crumbs, cheese, and the melted butter; sprinkle evenly over the casseroles. Bake, uncovered, at 375° for 15 minutes. Makes 2 servings.

Scallops Mornay

½ **cup dry white wine**
¼ **teaspoon salt**
   Dash white pepper
8 **ounces fresh** *or* **frozen**
   scallops
½ **cup sliced fresh mushrooms**
2 **tablespoons chopped onion**
1 **tablespoon butter** *or* **margarine**
4 **teaspoons all-purpose flour**
⅓ **cup milk**
¼ **cup shredded process Swiss**
   cheese (1 ounce)
2 **tablespoons snipped parsley**

In saucepan combine wine, salt, pepper, and ¾ cup water; bring to boiling. Add scallops and mushrooms; return to boiling. Cover; simmer till scallops are tender, about 5 minutes. Remove scallops and mushrooms; set aside. Boil liquid, uncovered, till reduced to ½ cup, 10 to 15 minutes.

In another saucepan cook onion in butter till tender; blend in flour. Add the ½ cup scallop liquid and milk. Cook and stir till thickened and bubbly. Stir in cheese till melted. Season with more salt and pepper, if needed. Remove from heat; stir in scallops and mushrooms. Turn into two 8- to 10-ounce individual casseroles. Bake, uncovered, at 375° for 15 to 20 minutes. Sprinkle with parsley. Serve with hot cooked rice, if desired. Makes 2 servings.

Tuna with Rice for One

1 small cucumber, seeded and
  chopped (½ cup)
1 3¼-ounce can tuna, drained
  and flaked *or* ½ cup flaked
  cooked fish
¼ cup quick-cooking rice
¼ cup water
1 teaspoon lemon juice
  Dash garlic salt
¼ cup shredded sharp American
  cheese (1 ounce)

In a 12-ounce casserole combine cucumber, tuna or fish, uncooked rice, water, lemon juice, and garlic salt. Bake, covered, at 350° till rice is cooked, about 25 minutes. Top with cheese. Bake, uncovered, till cheese melts, 2 to 3 minutes more. Makes 1 serving.
  Microwave cooking directions: In a 12-ounce nonmetal casserole combine cucumber, tuna or fish, uncooked rice, water, lemon juice, and garlic salt. Cook, covered with waxed paper, in a countertop microwave oven till rice is done, about 3 minutes. Sprinkle with cheese; micro-cook, uncovered, about 45 seconds longer.

Fiesta Salmon

½ of an 11-ounce can condensed
  Cheddar cheese soup
3 tablespoons milk
3 tablespoons chopped canned
  green chili peppers
2 teaspoons instant minced
  onion
1 7¾-ounce can salmon *or* 1 6½-
  or 7-ounce can tuna, drained
  and broken into chunks
¾ cup coarsely crushed
  tortilla chips

In a saucepan combine soup, milk, chili peppers, and onion. Heat and stir till bubbly. Stir in salmon or tuna and ½ *cup* of the corn chips. Turn mixture into two 8-ounce individual casseroles. Top with remaining tortilla chips. Bake, uncovered, at 375° till heated through, about 30 minutes. Makes 2 servings.

Stuffed Zucchini for One

1 small zucchini (6 inches long)
2 ounces bulk pork sausage
  (¼ cup)
1 tablespoon chopped onion
1 tablespoon chopped celery
¼ cup plain *or* garlic croutons
¼ cup shredded mozzarella *or*
  Monterey Jack cheese

Trim ends of zucchini; cook zucchini in boiling salted water till crisp-tender, about 8 minutes; drain. Cut in half lengthwise; scoop out centers and chop.
  Cook sausage, onion, and celery till meat is done; drain off fat. Stir in croutons, *half* the cheese, and the chopped zucchini. In a small baking dish mound mixture in zucchini shells. Bake, uncovered, at 350° for 20 minutes. Top with remaining cheese. Bake 5 minutes more. Makes 1 serving.

Pork Chop Supper (pictured on page 5)

2 pork chops, cut ¾ inch thick
⅓ cup regular rice
2 tablespoons chopped onion
1 cup water
1 teaspoon instant chicken
  bouillon granules
½ cup chopped apple
1 tablespoon butter, melted
1 tablespoon brown sugar
¼ teaspoon ground cinnamon
½ cup sliced apples

Trim fat from chops; cook trimmings in skillet till 2 tablespoons fat accumulates. Discard trimmings. Brown chops slowly in hot drippings. Set chops aside; reserve drippings.
  In same skillet cook rice and onion in reserved drippings till rice is golden, stirring constantly. Stir in water and bouillon granules. Bring to boiling; stir in chopped apple. Turn mixture into a 6½x6½x2-inch baking dish; arrange chops atop. Bake, covered, at 350° for 30 minutes. Combine butter, sugar, and cinnamon. Brush sliced apples with mixture; arrange around chops. Bake, uncovered, till apples and pork are tender, about 20 minutes. Serves 2.

3 For Entertaining

Good food and good company are the makings of a great party. And what better solution to menu problems than a casserole? You can create a masterpiece that guests will rave about and have plenty of time to socialize while dinner cooks, unwatched. In this chapter you'll find interesting food ideas—casseroles to impress discriminating guests, fun foods for informal entertaining, and recipes to prepare when you expect lots of people. It's up to you to provide the good company.

Plan a party around a festive casserole. *Mandarin Ham Rolls, Fruited Beef Stew,* and *Chicken Breasts Florentine* are three flavorful, attractive, and easy-to-serve alternatives.

Special Entrées

Chicken Breasts Florentine

2 10-ounce packages frozen chopped spinach
3 whole large chicken breasts, skinned, boned, and halved
1 rib celery, cut up
½ medium onion, cut up
½ teaspoon salt
¼ cup butter *or* margarine
¼ cup all-purpose flour
Dash white pepper
1 cup light cream
½ cup grated Parmesan cheese
Dash ground nutmeg

Cook spinach according to package directions; drain well.

Place chicken in saucepan with celery, onion, salt, and 1 cup water. Bring to boil; reduce heat and simmer till meat is tender, about 20 minutes. Remove chicken from broth. Strain broth; reserve 1 cup. Discard vegetables.

In saucepan melt butter; blend in flour and pepper. Stir in reserved broth and cream. Cook and stir till thickened and bubbly. Remove from heat; stir ½ *cup* of the sauce into drained spinach along with *half* the cheese and the nutmeg; spread in a 10x6x2-inch baking dish. Arrange chicken atop. Pour remaining sauce over all. Sprinkle with remaining cheese and more nutmeg, if desired. Bake, uncovered, at 375° till lightly browned, 25 to 30 minutes. Serves 6.

Mandarin Ham Rolls

1 11-ounce can mandarin orange sections, drained
1½ cups cooked rice
⅓ cup mayonnaise *or* salad dressing
2 tablespoons chopped pecans
2 tablespoons snipped parsley
1 tablespoon sliced green onion with tops
8 slices boiled ham (8 ounces)
¼ cup orange marmalade
1 tablespoon lemon juice
¼ teaspoon ground ginger

Reserve 8 orange sections; chop remainder and combine with cooked rice, mayonnaise, pecans, parsley, and onion. Divide mixture among ham slices. Roll up ham around filling. Place seam side down in 10x6x2-inch baking dish.

Combine marmalade, lemon juice, and ginger; brush some over ham rolls. Bake, uncovered, at 350° for 25 to 30 minutes, brushing occasionally with remaining sauce. Garnish with reserved orange sections. Makes 4 servings.

Fruited Beef Stew

1½ pounds boneless beef chuck, cut in 1-inch cubes
2 tablespoons cooking oil
3 medium sweet potatoes, peeled and quartered (3 cups)
1 16-ounce can tomatoes, cut up
1 cup chopped onion
½ cup chopped green pepper
2 inches stick cinnamon *or* ¼ teaspoon ground cinnamon
1 clove garlic, minced
1 teaspoon salt
⅛ teaspoon pepper
2 ears corn, cut crosswise in 2-inch pieces
2 medium zucchini, sliced
1 16-ounce can peach slices

In a Dutch oven brown meat, ⅓ at a time, in hot cooking oil. Drain off excess fat. Add sweet potatoes, undrained tomatoes, onion, green pepper, cinnamon, garlic, salt, pepper, and ½ cup water. (If desired, transfer mixture to a 3-quart casserole.) Bake, covered, at 350° for 1¼ hours. Stir in corn and zucchini; bake 45 minutes longer.

Drain peaches; reserve liquid for another use. Add peach slices to stew; season to taste with additional salt and pepper. Makes 6 to 8 servings.

Club Chicken Casserole (pictured on page 4)

2 cups chicken broth
⅔ cup regular rice
1 10-ounce package frozen
    chopped broccoli
3 tablespoons butter *or*
    margarine
3 tablespoons all-purpose flour
1½ teaspoons salt
    Dash pepper
2 cups milk
2 cups cubed cooked chicken
    or turkey
1 4½-ounce jar sliced mushrooms,
    drained
¼ cup toasted slivered almonds

In saucepan bring chicken broth and rice to boiling. Reduce heat; cook, covered, for 15 minutes. Remove from heat; let stand, covered, for 10 minutes. Meanwhile, cook broccoli according to package directions; drain well.

In saucepan melt butter or margarine. Stir in flour, salt, and pepper. Add milk all at once; cook and stir till thickened and bubbly. Stir in chicken, cooked rice, drained broccoli, and mushrooms. Turn into a 2-quart casserole. Bake, covered, at 350° till heated through, 30 to 35 minutes. Sprinkle with almonds. Makes 6 servings.

Saucy Turkey Manicotti

6 manicotti shells
2 tablespoons water
1 tablespoon instant minced
    onion
1 3-ounce package cream cheese,
    softened
1 1¼-ounce envelope sour
    cream sauce mix
¼ cup milk
1 4-ounce can chopped
    mushrooms, drained
1 tablespoon snipped parsley
¼ teaspoon salt
⅛ teaspoon pepper
2 cups chopped cooked turkey *or*
    chicken
1 1½-ounce envelope cheese
    sauce mix
¼ cup grated Parmesan cheese

Cook manicotti shells in boiling salted water till tender, 15 to 20 minutes; drain. Combine water and instant minced onion; let stand 5 minutes.

Combine cream cheese and sour cream sauce mix; blend in milk. Stir in softened onion, mushrooms, parsley, salt, and pepper. Add turkey or chicken; mix well. Spoon mixture into cooked manicotti shells. Arrange stuffed manicotti in a single layer in a 10x6x2-inch baking dish.

Prepare cheese sauce mix according to package directions. Pour sauce over manicotti. Sprinkle with Parmesan cheese. Bake, covered, at 350° till heated through, 35 to 40 minutes. Makes 6 servings.

Chicken Curry Soufflés

3 eggs, separated
1 cup cream-style cottage cheese
¼ cup finely chopped onion
1 clove garlic, minced
2 tablespoons butter *or*
    margarine
2 tablespoons all-purpose flour
1 teaspoon curry powder
½ teaspoon salt
¼ teaspoon ground ginger
½ cup milk
1 cup coarsely chopped cooked
    chicken *or* turkey

Beat egg whites till stiff peaks form; set aside. In another bowl beat together egg yolks and cottage cheese.

In a heavy saucepan cook onion and garlic in butter or margarine till onion is tender but not brown. Combine flour, curry, salt, and ginger; add to butter mixture, mixing well. Add milk all at once. Cook and stir till thickened and bubbly. Stir half the hot mixture into egg yolk mixture; return to pan. Cook and stir till thickened. Remove from heat; stir in chicken. Fold in beaten egg whites.

Turn mixture into four 8-ounce casseroles (or individual soufflé dishes with foil collars). Bake, uncovered, at 300° till a knife inserted off-center comes out clean, 40 to 45 minutes. Serve immediately. Makes 4 servings.

Crab-Stuffed Chicken

4 whole large chicken breasts, skinned, boned, and halved lengthwise
3 tablespoons butter *or* margarine
¼ cup all-purpose flour
¾ cup milk
¾ cup chicken broth
⅓ cup dry white wine
¼ cup chopped onion
1 tablespoon butter *or* margarine
1 7½-ounce can crab meat, drained, flaked, and cartilage removed
1 4-ounce can chopped mushrooms, drained
½ cup coarsely crumbled saltine crackers (10 crackers)
2 tablespoons snipped parsley
½ teaspoon salt
Dash pepper
1 cup shredded Swiss cheese
½ teaspoon paprika

Place one chicken piece, boned side up, between 2 pieces of waxed paper. Working from the center out, pound chicken lightly with meat mallet to make cutlet about ⅛ inch thick. Repeat with remaining chicken.

In saucepan melt the 3 tablespoons butter or margarine; blend in flour. Add milk, chicken broth, and wine all at once; cook and stir till thickened and bubbly. Set aside.

In skillet cook onion in the 1 tablespoon butter or margarine till tender but not brown. Stir in crab, mushrooms, cracker crumbs, parsley, salt, and pepper. Stir in *2 tablespoons* of the sauce. Top each chicken piece with about ¼ cup of the crab mixture. Fold sides in; roll up.

Place seam side down in a 12x7½x2-inch baking dish. Pour remaining sauce over all. Bake, covered, at 350° till chicken is tender, about 1 hour. Uncover; sprinkle with Swiss cheese and paprika. Bake till cheese melts, about 2 minutes longer. Makes 8 servings.

Chicken Divan

2 8-ounce packages frozen cut asparagus
1 10¾-ounce can condensed cream of chicken soup
1 teaspoon Worcestershire sauce
Dash ground nutmeg
½ cup grated Parmesan cheese
2 cups sliced cooked chicken
½ cup whipping cream
½ cup mayonnaise *or* salad dressing

Cook asparagus according to package directions; drain. Arrange in a 12x7½x2-inch baking dish.

Stir together soup, Worcestershire sauce, and nutmeg; pour *half* over asparagus. Sprinkle with ⅓ of the cheese. Top with chicken and remaining soup mixture. Sprinkle with another ⅓ of the cheese. Bake, uncovered, at 350° till heated through, about 20 minutes.

Whip cream just till soft peaks form; fold in mayonnaise. Spread mixture over chicken; sprinkle with remaining ⅓ of the cheese. Broil 3 to 4 inches from heat till topping is golden, 1 to 2 minutes. Makes 6 servings.

Wild Rice-Chicken Casserole

1 6-ounce package long grain and wild rice mix
½ cup chopped onion
½ cup chopped celery
2 tablespoons butter
1 10¾-ounce can condensed cream of mushroom soup
½ cup dairy sour cream
⅓ cup dry white wine
½ teaspoon curry powder
2 cups cubed cooked chicken *or* turkey
¼ cup snipped parsley

Prepare rice mix according to package directions. Meanwhile, cook onion and celery in butter till tender. Stir in soup, sour cream, wine, and curry. Stir in chicken and cooked rice; turn into a 12x7½x2-inch baking dish. Bake, uncovered, at 350° for 35 to 40 minutes. Stir before serving; garnish with snipped parsley. Makes 4 to 6 servings.

Microwave cooking directions: On range top prepare rice mix according to package directions. Place onion, celery, and butter in 2-quart nonmetal casserole. Cook, covered, in countertop microwave oven till tender, 2 to 2½ minutes. Blend in soup, sour cream, wine, and curry. Stir in chicken and rice. Micro-cook, covered, till hot, 8 to 10 minutes; turn dish after 5 minutes. Top with parsley.

Rice and Tuna Pie

1   beaten egg
2   cups cooked rice
2   tablespoons butter *or*
margarine, melted
2   tablespoons finely chopped
onion
½   teaspoon dried marjoram,
crushed
1   9¼-ounce can tuna, drained
and flaked
3   beaten eggs
1   cup milk
1   cup shredded Swiss cheese
(4 ounces)
¼   teaspoon salt
Dash pepper

Combine the 1 egg, cooked rice, melted butter, *1 tablespoon* of the chopped onion, and *¼ teaspoon* of the marjoram. Press onto bottom and sides of a lightly buttered 10-inch pie plate or 10x6x2-inch baking dish. Place tuna atop.

Combine the 3 beaten eggs, milk, Swiss cheese, salt, pepper, remaining 1 tablespoon onion, and remaining ¼ teaspoon marjoram. Pour over tuna. Bake, uncovered, at 350° till a knife inserted just off-center comes out clean, 40 to 45 minutes. Garnish with chopped pimiento or snipped parsley, if desired. Makes 6 servings.

Curried Eggs with Shrimp

8   hard-cooked eggs
⅓   cup mayonnaise
½   teaspoon salt
½   teaspoon paprika
¼   teaspoon curry powder
¼   teaspoon dry mustard
2   tablespoons butter *or*
margarine
2   tablespoons all-purpose flour
¼   teaspoon curry powder
1   10¾-ounce can condensed
cream of celery soup
¾   cup milk
1   cup frozen cooked shrimp
½   cup shredded sharp Cheddar
cheese (2 ounces)
¾   cup soft bread crumbs
1   tablespoon butter *or*
margarine, melted

Cut eggs in half lengthwise; remove and mash yolks. Mix mashed yolks with mayonnaise, salt, paprika, the ¼ teaspoon curry powder, and dry mustard. Stuff egg whites with yolk mixture. Arrange egg halves in a 10x6x2-inch baking dish.

Melt the 2 tablespoons butter; blend in flour and the ¼ teaspoon curry powder. Add soup and milk; cook and stir till thickened and bubbly. Add shrimp and cheese; stir till cheese melts. Pour sauce over eggs in baking dish.

Toss bread crumbs with the melted butter to combine; sprinkle around edge of mixture. Bake, uncovered, at 350° till heated through, 15 to 20 minutes. Makes 6 to 8 servings.

Menu-Planning Reminders

Menu planning is easy when you serve a casserole. Since a casserole is a combination of foods, you can keep accompaniments simple—serve a plain vegetable or salad with a casserole entrée, a vegetable casserole with a simple entrée.

Use a variety of colors, flavors, textures, and temperatures to make a menu more interesting. Choose attractive foods; and remember that a garnish of parsley or toasted almonds can transform a plain dish into an elegant one.

When your budget won't allow you to stage a spectacular party with all the trimmings, invite a few friends over for *Highbrow Haddock.* And don't tell them how inexpensive it is.

Highbrow Haddock

1 **pound frozen haddock fillets**
¼ **cup finely chopped onion**
¼ **cup butter** *or* **margarine**
2 **tablespoons all-purpose flour**
¼ **teaspoon salt**
⅛ **teaspoon pepper**
1½ **cups milk**
1 **cup shredded sharp American cheese (4 ounces)**
1 **1¼-ounce envelope sour cream sauce mix**
1 **cup frozen peas, thawed**
1 **4-ounce can mushroom stems and pieces, drained**
1½ **cups soft bread crumbs**

In large skillet barely cover haddock with water. Simmer gently till fish flakes with a fork, 12 to 15 minutes; drain. Break fish into large chunks; set aside.

Meanwhile, in large saucepan cook onion in *2 tablespoons* of the butter or margarine till tender but not brown. Blend in flour, salt, and pepper. Add *1 cup* of the milk all at once. Cook and stir till thickened and bubbly. Remove from heat. Add cheese; stir till melted.

Using the remaining ½ cup milk, prepare sauce mix according to package directions. Stir in cheese sauce, fish, peas, and mushrooms. Turn into six 8-ounce shallow casseroles. Melt remaining 2 tablespons butter; toss with bread crumbs to combine. Sprinkle atop casseroles. Bake, uncovered, at 400° for 15 to 20 minutes. Garnish each with parsley and paprika, if desired. Makes 6 servings.

After a day of skiing or sledding, you're bound to be cold and weary. Take the chill
off with corn bread and *Easy Cassoulet,* a hearty mixture of ham, beans, wine, and seasonings.

Shrimp Tartlets

Plain Pastry (see page 12)
3 eggs
1½ cups cream-style cottage
    cheese (12 ounces)
1 8½-ounce can peas, drained
½ teaspoon salt
    Dash pepper
1 4½-ounce can shrimp, drained
    and rinsed (about 1 cup)

Prepare Plain Pastry; divide into four parts. On floured surface roll out into four 7-inch circles. Fit pastry rounds into four 5-inch tart pans; flute edges. Set aside.

Beat eggs till foamy; stir in cottage cheese, peas, salt, and pepper. Reserve 4 shrimp for garnish; stir remaining into egg mixture. Turn into prepared pastry shells. Bake, uncovered, at 350° till a knife inserted off-center comes out clean, about 40 minutes. Let stand 5 minutes. Garnish with reserved shrimp and parsley, if desired. Makes 4 servings.

Hot Crab Bake

6 tablespoons butter *or*
    margarine
¼ cup all-purpose flour
2 cups milk
1 7½-ounce can crab meat,
    drained, flaked, and
    cartilage removed
2 hard-cooked eggs, chopped
½ cup chopped pimiento
½ cup fine dry bread crumbs
¼ cup slivered almonds

In skillet melt *4 tablespoons* of the butter; blend in flour. Add milk all at once; cook and stir till thickened and bubbly. Stir in crab meat, chopped eggs, pimiento, 1 teaspoon salt, and ⅛ teaspoon pepper. Spoon mixture into 6 individual casseroles or baking shells.

Melt remaining 2 tablespoons butter; toss with bread crumbs to combine. Sprinkle crumbs atop crab mixture. Top with slivered almonds. Bake, uncovered, at 350° for 20 to 25 minutes. Makes 6 servings.

Easy Cassoulet

½ pound bulk pork sausage
1 small onion, sliced (½ cup)
1 clove garlic, minced
1½ cups cubed fully cooked ham
2 tablespoons snipped parsley
1 bay leaf
2 15-ounce cans navy beans
¼ cup dry white wine
    Dash ground cloves

In skillet cook sausage, onion, and garlic till meat is lightly browned and onion is tender; drain off fat.

Add ham, parsley, and bay leaf; mix well. Stir in undrained beans, wine, and cloves. Turn into a 1½-quart casserole. Bake, covered, at 325° for 45 minutes. Uncover and bake 40 to 45 minutes longer, stirring occasionally. Remove bay leaf. Serve in bowls with hot corn bread, if desired. Makes 6 servings.

Shallot-Bacon Quiche

6 slices bacon
¼ cup sliced shallots (4 medium)
    Plain Pastry (see page 12)
1 cup shredded Swiss cheese
3 beaten eggs
1 cup light cream
½ teaspoon salt
½ teaspoon dry mustard
    Dash ground nutmeg

In skillet cook bacon till crisp; drain, reserving 1 tablespoon drippings. Cook shallots in reserved drippings till tender.

Prepare Plain Pastry. Roll out and fit into an 8-inch pie plate or quiche dish; flute edges. Bake at 450° for 5 minutes; set aside. Reduce oven temperature to 325°.

Sprinkle cheese over pastry. Crumble bacon over cheese; top with shallots. Combine remaining ingredients; pour over mixture in pastry. Bake, uncovered, at 325° till set, 40 to 45 minutes. Let stand 10 minutes. Makes 6 servings.

Cauliflower-Ham Bake

1   large head cauliflower
2   tablespoons butter *or* margarine
3   tablespoons all-purpose flour
1½ cups milk
1½ cups shredded sharp American cheese (6 ounces)
2   cups cubed fully cooked ham
1   4-ounce can mushroom stems and pieces, drained
¼   cup fine dry bread crumbs
1   tablespoon butter *or* margarine, melted

Break cauliflower into flowerets (should have about 5 cups); cook in boiling salted water till tender, about 10 minutes. Drain thoroughly; set aside.

In saucepan melt the 2 tablespoons butter or margarine. Stir in flour; add milk all at once. Cook and stir till thickened and bubbly. Add cheese and stir till melted. Stir in cooked cauliflower, ham, and mushrooms. Turn into a 2-quart casserole. Combine crumbs and the melted butter; sprinkle over top. Bake, uncovered, at 350° till heated through, 30 to 35 minutes. Makes 6 servings.

Gold Rush Brunch

1   5½-ounce package dry hash brown potatoes with onion
¼   cup butter *or* margarine
¼   cup all-purpose flour
½   teaspoon salt
⅛   teaspoon pepper
2   cups milk
1   cup dairy sour cream
2   tablespoons snipped parsley
8   slices Canadian-style bacon, cut ¼ inch thick
8   eggs

Prepare potatoes according to package directions; set aside. In 3-quart saucepan melt butter; blend in flour, salt, and pepper. Add milk all at once; cook and stir till thickened and bubbly. Remove from heat. Stir in sour cream, parsley, and potatoes.

Turn mixture into a 13x9x2-inch baking dish. Arrange Canadian-style bacon in a row down center, overlapping slices slightly. Bake, uncovered, at 350° for 20 minutes.

Remove from oven. Make 4 depressions in potato mixture on *each* side of the row of bacon; slip 1 egg into each depression. Sprinkle with salt and pepper. Return to oven; bake till eggs are set, 10 to 12 minutes more. Makes 8 servings.

Pizza Quiche

2   recipes Plain Pastry (see page 12)
1   cup ricotta *or* cream-style cottage cheese (8 ounces)
3   eggs
4   ounces Italian sausage, cooked and drained
1   cup shredded mozzarella cheese (4 ounces)
½   cup sliced pepperoni, halved (2 ounces)
½   cup cubed prosciutto *or* fully cooked ham
½   cup sliced salami, cut in strips (2 ounces)
¼   cup grated Parmesan cheese
1   beaten egg
2   tablespoons milk

Prepare Plain Pastry. Divide dough in half. Roll out half; fit into a 9-inch pie plate. Reserve remaining dough. Crimp edges of pastry shell; *do not prick.* Bake at 450° for 5 minutes. Remove from oven; reduce oven temperature to 350°.

Beat together ricotta or cottage cheese and the 3 eggs; fold in Italian sausage, mozzarella, pepperoni, prosciutto or ham, salami, and Parmesan cheese. Turn into partially baked pastry shell.

Roll out remaining pastry dough to an 8-inch circle; cut in 6 to 8 wedges. Arrange wedges atop filling. Bake, uncovered, at 350° for 20 minutes.

Combine the 1 egg and milk; brush over pastry wedges. Continue baking till golden brown, about 20 minutes more. Let stand about 10 minutes before serving. Makes 6 to 8 servings.

Spinach and Cheese Soufflé

1 10-ounce package frozen
  chopped spinach
¼ cup butter *or* margarine
¼ cup all-purpose flour
½ teaspoon salt
1 cup milk
1 cup shredded sharp American
  cheese (4 ounces)
4 egg yolks
4 stiffly beaten egg whites
½ cup milk
  Dash white pepper
¼ cup dairy sour cream

Cook spinach according to package directions; drain well. In saucepan melt butter. Blend in flour and salt. Add the 1 cup milk all at once. Cook and stir till thickened and bubbly. Remove from heat. Add cheese; stir till melted. Reserve ¾ *cup* of the sauce; stir spinach into remaining sauce.

Beat egg yolks till thick and lemon-colored, about 5 minutes. Slowly stir in spinach mixture; gradually pour over beaten egg whites, folding together well. Turn into a 1½-quart soufflé dish. Bake, uncovered, at 350° till knife inserted just off-center comes out clean, 30 to 35 minutes. Just before serving, in saucepan combine reserved sauce, the ½ cup milk, and pepper; heat till bubbly. Slowly stir hot sauce into sour cream. Pass with soufflé. Makes 4 to 6 servings.

Party Eggplant Parmesan

¾ cup soft bread crumbs
  (1 slice)
⅓ cup milk
1 teaspoon seasoned salt
½ teaspoon seasoned pepper
1 pound ground beef
½ pound ground veal
  Cooking oil
1 medium eggplant
¼ cup all-purpose flour
2 8-ounce cans tomato sauce
  with mushrooms
¼ cup water
¼ teaspoon dried oregano,
  crushed
½ cup grated Parmesan cheese

Combine crumbs, milk, salt, and pepper. Add beef and veal; mix well. Shape into 8 patties. Brown on both sides in a small amount of cooking oil. Remove from skillet.

Peel eggplant; cut into eight thick slices. Brush lightly with oil; coat with flour. Brown eggplant slices in same skillet. Arrange slices in a 13x9x2-inch baking pan; top each slice with a meat patty.

Combine tomato sauce, water, and oregano; pour over all. Sprinkle with Parmesan cheese. Bake, uncovered, at 350° for 20 to 25 minutes. Makes 8 servings.

Beef-Broccoli Pie

1 pound ground beef
¼ cup chopped onion
2 tablespoons all-purpose flour
¾ teaspoon salt
¼ teaspoon garlic salt
1¼ cups milk
1 3-ounce package cream
  cheese, softened
1 beaten egg
1 10-ounce package frozen
  chopped broccoli, cooked
  and well drained
2 recipes Plain Pastry (see
  page 12)
4 ounces Monterey Jack cheese,
  sliced
  Milk

In a skillet brown beef and onion; drain off fat. Stir in flour, salt, and garlic salt. Add 1¼ cups milk and the softened cream cheese; cook and stir till smooth and bubbly. Stir about 1 cup of the hot mixture into the beaten egg; return to mixture in skillet. Cook and stir over medium heat till mixture is thickened, 1 to 2 minutes. Stir in cooked chopped broccoli; set aside.

Prepare Plain Pastry as for a double-crust pie. Spoon the hot meat mixture into the pastry shell. Arrange cheese slices atop the meat mixture. Adjust remaining pastry over filling to form the top crust; crimp edges to seal. Cut slashes for escape of steam.

Brush top crust with a little milk. Bake, uncovered, at 350° for 40 to 45 minutes. If the pastry browns too quickly, cover edges of crust with foil during last 20 minutes of baking. Let stand 10 minutes. Makes 6 servings.

Sherried Beef Stroganoff

2 pounds beef stew meat, cut
   in 1-inch cubes
¼ cup all-purpose flour
2 tablespoons cooking oil
1 10¾-ounce can condensed
   cream of mushroom soup
½ cup dry sherry
1 1½-ounce envelope stroganoff
   sauce mix
1 tablespoon instant minced
   onion
1 4-ounce can sliced mushrooms,
   drained
½ cup dairy sour cream

Toss beef cubes with flour to coat. In large skillet brown meat in hot cooking oil. Drain off excess fat.

Combine soup, sherry, dry stroganoff sauce mix, and instant minced onion; stir into meat along with mushrooms. Turn mixture into a 2-quart casserole. Bake, covered, at 350° till meat is tender, about 1½ hours. Stir in sour cream. Serve over hot cooked white or brown rice, if desired. Makes 6 to 8 servings.

Beef Burgundy Pies

1½ pounds beef stew meat, cut in
   1-inch cubes
2 tablespoons cooking oil
1½ cups water
1 beef bouillon cube
1 cup sliced carrot
¾ cup chopped onion
2 cloves garlic, minced
½ cup Burgundy
¼ cup all-purpose flour
1 teaspoon Worcestershire sauce
½ teaspoon salt
½ teaspoon mixed salad herbs
½ teaspoon Kitchen Bouquet
⅛ teaspoon pepper
1 cup packaged biscuit mix
⅓ cup water

In a 3-quart saucepan brown meat in hot cooking oil. Drain off fat. Add the 1½ cups water and bouillon cube. Bring to boiling. Cover; reduce heat and simmer over low heat for 30 minutes.

Add sliced carrot, chopped onion, and minced garlic; simmer till meat is tender, about 20 minutes longer. Blend Burgundy into flour; slowly stir into hot meat mixture. Add Worcestershire sauce, salt, mixed salad herbs, Kitchen Bouquet, and pepper to beef mixture. Cook and stir till thickened and bubbly. Turn into four 8-ounce casseroles.

Stir together biscuit mix and the ⅓ cup water; drop from a spoon atop the *hot* meat mixture in each casserole. Bake, uncovered, at 375° till biscuits are golden brown, 15 to 20 minutes. Makes 4 servings.

Curried Beef Bake

2 tablespoons all-purpose flour
½ teaspoon salt
   Dash pepper
1 pound beef stew meat, cut in
   ½-inch cubes
2 tablespoons cooking oil
1 tablespoon instant minced
   onion
1 5½-ounce package noodles with
   sour cream mix
1 8-ounce can tomato sauce
2 tablespoons butter *or*
   margarine
1½ teaspoons curry powder
⅓ cup finely crushed rich round
   crackers (8 crackers)

In paper or plastic bag combine flour, salt, and pepper. Add beef cubes, a few at a time; shake to coat. In a large skillet brown meat in hot oil. Remove from heat. Drain off excess fat. To skillet add instant minced onion and 2¼ cups water; cover and simmer for 30 minutes.

Meanwhile, cook noodles from the mix in large amount boiling salted water for 5 minutes; drain. In same saucepan blend sauce mix, tomato sauce, butter, and curry. Stir in meat mixture; fold in cooked noodles.

Turn mixture into a 1½-quart casserole. Bake, covered, at 350° for 30 minutes. Uncover and sprinkle with cracker crumbs; bake till crumbs are lightly browned, about 10 minutes longer. Makes 4 servings.

Tetrazzini Crepes (pictured on page 4)

12 **Crepes (see recipe below)**
5 **ounces fresh mushrooms,**
   halved (2 cups)
6 **tablespoons butter *or***
   margarine
⅓ **cup all-purpose flour**
1¼ **cups chicken broth**
¾ **cup light cream**
½ **cup shredded sharp Cheddar**
   cheese (2 ounces)
¼ **cup dry sherry**
2 **cups cubed cooked chicken**
   ***or* turkey**
2 **tablespoons chopped pitted**
   ripe olives
2 **tablespoons snipped parsley**

Prepare Crepes. Brown mushroom halves in *3 tablespoons* of the butter or margarine.

In saucepan melt the remaining 3 tablespoons butter; stir in flour. Add chicken broth and cream. Cook and stir till mixture is thickened and bubbly. Add cheese and sherry; stir till cheese melts.

Combine chicken, olives, mushrooms, and *1 cup* of the sauce. Spoon about ¼ cup filling on unbrowned side of each crepe; roll up. Place crepes seam side up in a 13x9x2-inch baking dish or two 10x6x2-inch baking dishes; pour remaining sauce over. Bake, uncovered, at 375° till heated through, about 25 minutes for the 13x9x2-inch dish or 20 minutes for the two 10x6x2-inch dishes. Sprinkle with parsley. Serves 6.

Salmon-Broccoli Crepes

12 **Crepes (see recipe below)**
¼ **cup chopped onion**
¼ **cup butter *or* margarine**
¼ **cup all-purpose flour**
¼ **teaspoon salt**
2¼ **cups milk**
2 **cups shredded sharp American**
   cheese (8 ounces)
1 **10-ounce package frozen**
   chopped broccoli
1 **7¾-ounce can salmon, drained,**
   boned, and flaked

Prepare Crepes; set aside. In saucepan cook onion in butter till tender but not brown. Stir in flour and salt. Add milk; cook and stir till thickened and bubbly. Add cheese; stir till melted. Remove from heat.

Cook broccoli according to package directions; drain. Cut up any large pieces; fold in salmon and ¾ *cup* of the sauce. Spoon about 3 tablespoons salmon mixture onto unbrowned side of each crepe; roll up. Place crepes seam side down in a 12x7½x2-inch baking dish; pour remaining sauce over crepes. Bake, covered, at 375° till heated through, 20 to 25 minutes. Makes 4 to 6 servings.

Crepes

1 **cup all-purpose flour**
1½ **cups milk**
2 **eggs**
1 **tablespoon cooking oil**
¼ **teaspoon salt**

In a bowl combine flour, milk, eggs, oil, and salt; beat with a rotary beater till blended. Heat a lightly greased 6-inch skillet; remove from heat. Spoon in about 2 tablespoons batter; lift and tilt skillet to spread evenly. Return to heat; brown on one side only. To remove, invert pan over paper toweling. Repeat with remaining batter to make 12 crepes, greasing skillet occasionally.

Make Casseroles Ahead

Shorten the time you'll spend in the kitchen after your guests arrive—prepare a casserole the day before.

Assemble the casserole as directed, but omit the final heating step. Cover the dish tightly and store it in the refrigerator. Be sure to use within one or two days. When you heat the casserole, remember to allow an extra 15 to 20 minutes of baking time for the chilled food to heat through.

Casseroles for a Crowd

Hamburger-Noodle Bake

4 **pounds ground beef**
3 **large onions, chopped (3 cups)**
1 **cup chopped green pepper**
16 **ounces medium noodles**
3 **10¾-ounce cans condensed
     tomato soup**
4 **cups shredded American cheese**
1 **12-ounce bottle chili sauce**
¼ **cup chopped pimiento**
2 **teaspoons salt**
2 **teaspoons chili powder**
½ **teaspoon pepper**
4½ **cups soft bread crumbs**
¼ **cup butter, melted**

In a large skillet cook beef, onion, and green pepper, half at a time, till meat is brown. Drain off fat.

Cook noodles according to package directions; drain well. Return drained noodles to kettle. Stir in meat mixture, tomato soup, cheese, chili sauce, pimiento, salt, chili powder, pepper, and 2 cups water; mix well. Divide mixture between two 13x9x2-inch baking dishes.

Toss bread crumbs with melted butter; sprinkle atop casseroles. Bake, uncovered, at 350° till heated through, about 45 minutes. Garnish with green pepper rings, if desired. Makes 2 casseroles, 12 servings each.

Layered Supper

4 **pounds potatoes, peeled and
     thinly sliced (12 cups)**
2 **17-ounce cans whole kernel
     corn, drained**
1 **cup chopped green pepper**
2 **cups chopped onion (2 large)**
4 **cups sliced carrot (8 medium)**
3 **pounds ground beef**
1 **15-ounce can tomato sauce**
2 **cups shredded sharp American
     cheese (8 ounces)**

Divide potatoes between two 12x7½x2-inch baking dishes. Season with salt and pepper. Arrange corn and green pepper over potatoes in each casserole. Layer the onion, then the carrot in each. Crumble beef evenly over the vegetables; sprinkle with more salt and pepper. Pat gently to smooth. Top each casserole with tomato sauce.

Bake, covered, at 350° for 2 hours. Uncover; sprinkle with cheese. Let stand 10 to 15 minutes before serving. Makes 2 casseroles, 8 or 9 servings each.

Barbecued Beans and Meatballs

3 **beaten eggs**
⅔ **cup milk**
2 **tablespoons instant minced
     onion**
3 **cups soft bread crumbs**
3 **pounds ground beef**
2 **31-ounce cans pork and beans
     in tomato sauce**
1 **28-ounce can tomatoes, cut up**
2 **12-ounce cans whole kernel
     corn, drained**
1 **8-ounce can tomato sauce**
¼ **cup packed brown sugar**
¼ **cup light molasses**
2 **tablespoons prepared mustard**
8 **fully cooked smoked sausage
     links *or* frankfurters**
2 **cups shredded American cheese**

In a large bowl combine eggs, milk, and instant minced onion; let stand 5 minutes. Stir in bread crumbs, 1½ teaspoons salt, and ¼ teaspoon pepper. Add ground beef; mix well. With wet hands, shape mixture into 48 two-inch meatballs. Place meatballs in two 15½x10½x1-inch baking pans. Bake, uncovered, at 375° for 20 minutes. Drain off fat.

Meanwhile, in a large Dutch oven combine pork and beans, tomatoes, corn, tomato sauce, brown sugar, molasses, and mustard. Heat till boiling.

Cut sausages or frankfurters crosswise into thirds. Divide sausages and meatballs between two 3-quart casseroles. Turn *half* the bean mixture into *each* casserole. Stir to combine. Bake, uncovered, at 375° for 1½ hours, stirring occasionally. Sprinkle with cheese. Bake till cheese melts, 2 to 3 minutes longer. Makes 2 casseroles, 12 servings each.

Next time it's your turn to serve two football teams (or six tables of bridge), don't panic. Put *Hamburger-Noodle Bake* in the oven about 45 minutes before you plan to eat, then relax.

Ham and Broccoli Bake

2 20-ounce packages frozen
   cut broccoli
1 large onion, chopped (1 cup)
¼ cup butter *or* margarine
2 10¾-ounce cans condensed
   cream of mushroom soup
2 10¾-ounce cans condensed
   cream of celery soup
2 soup cans milk (2½ cups)
2 cups shredded sharp American
   cheese (8 ounces)
6 cups cubed fully cooked ham
4 cups quick-cooking rice
1 tablespoon Worcestershire
   sauce

Cook frozen broccoli according to package directions; drain well. In saucepan cook onion in butter or margarine till tender but not brown.

In a large mixing bowl stir together mushroom soup, celery soup, milk, and cheese. Add drained broccoli, cooked onion, ham, uncooked rice, and Worcestershire sauce; mix well. Divide mixture between two 2½-quart casseroles.

Bake, covered, at 350° till rice is done, 45 to 50 minutes. Garnish each with a sprig of watercress, if desired. Makes 2 casseroles, 10 servings each.

Peppy Lasagna

1 pound bulk Italian sausage
½ cup chopped onion
½ cup chopped celery
½ cup chopped carrot
1 16-ounce can tomatoes, cut up
1 6-ounce can tomato paste
1 teaspoon sugar
½ teaspoon dried oregano,
   crushed
10 ounces lasagna noodles
2 beaten eggs
2 cups ricotta *or* cream-style
   cottage cheese (16 ounces)
½ cup grated Parmesan cheese
2 tablespoons snipped parsley
16 ounces mozzarella cheese,
   thinly sliced

In a large skillet cook sausage, onion, celery, and carrot till meat is lightly browned. Drain off excess fat. Stir in tomatoes, tomato paste, sugar, oregano, 1 teaspoon salt, and ¼ teaspoon pepper. Simmer, uncovered, for 20 minutes, stirring occasionally.

Meanwhile, cook lasagna noodles according to package directions; drain well. Combine eggs, ricotta, Parmesan cheese, parsley, and ¼ teaspoon pepper.

Arrange *half* the lasagna noodles in a greased 13x9x2-inch baking dish. Spread with *half* the cheese filling; add *half* the mozzarella cheese and *half* the meat sauce. Repeat layers. Bake, uncovered, at 375° till bubbly, about 40 minutes. Let stand 10 to 15 minutes. Makes 12 servings.

Sausage au Gratin

4 pounds potatoes (12 medium)
2 8-ounce jars cheese spread
2 cups dairy sour cream
2 tablespoons instant minced
   onion
1 tablespoon dried parsley flakes
1 12-ounce package fully cooked
   smoked sausage links, sliced
1½ cups soft bread crumbs
1 tablespoon melted butter
¼ teaspoon paprika

In covered kettle cook potatoes in boiling salted water to cover till tender, about 30 minutes. Drain and cool. When cool enough to handle, peel and slice potatoes.

Meanwhile, in a large bowl blend together cheese spread and sour cream. Stir in instant minced onion, parsley flakes, and 1 teaspoon salt. Fold in sliced potatoes and sliced sausages. Turn into a 13x9x2-inch baking dish. Bake, uncovered, at 350° for 40 to 45 minutes.

Toss together bread crumbs, melted butter, and paprika. Sprinkle atop casserole. Bake till lightly browned, about 10 minutes longer. Makes 12 servings.

Rich and creamy *Ham and Broccoli Bake* is ideal for a spur-of-the-moment get-together.
Share it with as many as 20 friends and relatives, or halve the recipe to serve a smaller group.

Casserole Chop Suey

5 **pounds boneless pork, cut in**
  ½-inch cubes
2 **tablespoons cooking oil**
1 **teaspoon salt**
4 **10¾-ounce cans condensed**
  cream of mushroom soup
4 **cups milk**
1 **16-ounce can bean sprouts,**
  drained
1½ **cups chopped celery**
1½ **cups chopped onion**
1½ **cups chopped green pepper**
1½ **cups regular rice**
1 **8-ounce can water chestnuts,**
  drained and sliced
⅔ **cup soy sauce**
2 **3-ounce cans chow mein noodles**

In a large kettle or Dutch oven brown meat, about ⅓ at a time, in hot oil. Return meat to pan; sprinkle with salt. Stir in soup, milk, bean sprouts, celery, onion, green pepper, uncooked rice, water chestnuts, and soy sauce. Divide mixture between two 13x9x2-inch baking dishes.

Bake, covered, at 350° till rice is done, about 1½ hours, stirring after 1 hour. Uncover; stir each casserole. Sprinkle *each* with 1 can of chow mein noodles. Bake 5 minutes longer. Pass additional soy sauce with casseroles. Makes 2 casseroles, 12 servings each.

Spinach Squares Hollandaise

3 **10-ounce packages frozen
  chopped spinach**
½ **cup finely chopped onion**
2 **tablespoons butter *or*
  margarine**
4 **beaten eggs**
2 **cups milk**
3 **cups soft bread crumbs**
3 **cups chopped fully cooked ham**
½ **teaspoon seasoned salt**
2 **1⅛-ounce envelopes
  hollandaise sauce mix**
4 **hard-cooked eggs, chopped**

Cook frozen spinach according to package directions; drain well. Cook chopped onion in butter or margarine till onion is tender but not brown. Combine beaten eggs and milk. Add bread crumbs, ham, cooked onion, spinach, and seasoned salt; mix well. Spread evenly in a 12x7½x2-inch baking dish. Bake, uncovered, at 350° till set, 40 to 45 minutes.

Meanwhile, prepare hollandaise sauce mix according to package directions; stir in chopped hard-cooked eggs.

To serve, cut casserole into squares; spoon sauce over each serving. Makes 12 servings.

Ham Potluck Supper

½ **cup chopped onion**
½ **cup chopped green pepper**
¼ **cup butter *or* margarine**
⅓ **cup all-purpose flour**
2 **10½-ounce cans condensed
  chicken with rice soup**
1 **cup milk**
3 **cups cubed fully cooked ham**
7 **hard-cooked eggs, sliced**
1½ **cups soft bread crumbs**
2 **tablespoons butter, melted**

Cook onion and green pepper in the ¼ cup butter or margarine till tender but not brown. Blend in flour; stir in soup and milk. Cook and stir till thickened and bubbly. Fold in ham and *six* of the sliced hard-cooked eggs. Turn mixture into a 12x7½x2-inch baking dish.

Toss bread crumbs with melted butter to combine. Sprinkle around edges of baking dish. Bake, uncovered, at 350° for 25 minutes. Top with remaining egg slices. Makes 10 servings.

Seafood Lasagna

8 **lasagna noodles**
1 **large onion, chopped (1 cup)**
2 **tablespoons butter**
1 **8-ounce package cream
  cheese, softened**
1½ **cups cream-style cottage
  cheese (12 ounces)**
1 **beaten egg**
2 **teaspoons dried basil, crushed**
½ **teaspoon salt**
⅛ **teaspoon pepper**
2 **10¾-ounce cans condensed
  cream of mushroom soup**
⅓ **cup milk**
⅓ **cup dry white wine**
1 **pound fresh *or* frozen shelled
  shrimp, cooked and halved**
1 **7½-ounce can crab meat,
  drained, flaked, and
  cartilage removed**
¼ **cup grated Parmesan cheese**
½ **cup shredded sharp American
  cheese (2 ounces)**

Cook lasagna noodles according to package directions; drain well. Arrange 4 noodles to cover bottom of a greased 13x9x2-inch baking dish.

Cook onion in butter till tender but not brown; blend in cream cheese. Stir in cottage cheese, egg, basil, salt, and pepper; spread *half* atop noodles.

Combine soup, milk, and wine. Stir in shrimp and crab; spread *half* over cottage cheese layer.

Repeat layers of noodles, cheese mixture, and seafood mixture. Sprinkle with Parmesan cheese. Bake, uncovered, at 350° for 45 minutes. Top with shredded American cheese. Bake till cheese melts, 2 to 3 minutes more. Let stand 15 minutes before serving. Makes 12 servings.

Crowd-Size Chicken Bake

16 ounces medium noodles
½ cup butter *or* margarine
½ cup all-purpose flour
1½ teaspoons salt
¼ teaspoon white pepper
7 cups milk
4 10½-ounce cans chicken gravy
8 cups chopped cooked chicken
   or turkey
1 2-ounce jar diced pimiento,
   drained (¼ cup)
1 cup fine dry bread crumbs
¼ cup butter *or* margarine,
   melted

Cook noodles according to package directions; drain well. In a large kettle melt the ½ cup butter or margarine. Blend in flour, salt, and pepper. Add milk all at once. Cook and stir till thickened and bubbly; stir in chicken gravy. Stir in chicken or turkey, pimiento, and cooked noodles. Divide mixture between two 13x9x2-inch baking dishes. Bake, covered, at 350° about 35 minutes.

Toss together bread crumbs and the melted butter to combine; sprinkle atop casseroles. Bake, uncovered, 10 minutes longer. Makes 2 casseroles, 12 servings each.

Buffet Chicken Scallop

1 cup regular rice
1 large onion, chopped (1 cup)
1 cup chopped green pepper
2 tablespoons butter *or*
   margarine
1 16-ounce package herb-
   seasoned stuffing mix
4 cups chicken broth
6 beaten eggs
3 10¾-ounce cans condensed
   cream of celery soup
8 cups chopped cooked chicken
   or turkey
1 4-ounce jar diced pimiento,
   drained (½ cup)
2 10¾-ounce cans condensed
   cream of chicken soup
½ cup milk
1 cup dairy sour cream

Cook rice according to package directions. Meanwhile, cook chopped onion and green pepper in butter or margarine till tender but not brown.

In large mixing bowl combine stuffing mix with broth; stir in eggs and celery soup; add chicken, cooked rice, onion-green pepper mixture, and pimiento. Mix well. Divide between two greased 13x9x2-inch baking dishes. Bake, uncovered, at 325° for 30 to 40 minutes.

In saucepan combine chicken soup and milk; heat and stir till smooth. Stir in sour cream; heat through but *do not boil.* To serve, cut casserole into squares; spoon sauce over each serving. Makes 2 casseroles, 12 servings each.

Turkey with Fruited Stuffing

1 2½-pound frozen boneless
   turkey roast
1 cup chopped celery
½ cup butter *or* margarine
1 cup pitted dried prunes,
   chopped
½ cup water*
½ teaspoon ground sage
1 8-ounce package corn bread
   stuffing mix
1 cup orange juice
¼ cup water
1 tablespoon cornstarch
1 tablespoon soy sauce

Cook turkey roast according to package directions. In large saucepan cook celery in butter or margarine till tender. Stir in prunes, the ½ cup water, and sage. Add stuffing mix; toss to coat. Turn mixture into a 12x7½x2-inch baking dish.

Cut turkey roast into 10 slices; arrange atop stuffing mixture. Bake, covered, at 350° for 30 to 35 minutes.

Meanwhile, in saucepan slowly stir orange juice and the ¼ cup water into cornstarch. Stir in soy sauce; cook and stir till thickened and bubbly. Pour orange sauce over turkey. Makes 10 servings.

*Increase water to ¾ cup if moister stuffing is desired.

4 International Specialties

Ready to embark on a culinary adventure? Sample dishes from around the world and discover the seasonings that typify each area: saffron from Spain, cinnamon from Greece, chilies from Latin America, and garlic from Italy. Enjoy these casseroles—the best of international cooking.

Of French origin, *Quiche Lorraine* is a main-dish custard tart flavored with Swiss cheese and bacon. Serve it as an entrée, or cut the pie in smaller wedges for an appetizer.

Quiche Lorraine (French)

Plain Pastry (see page 12)
4 slices bacon
1 cup shredded Swiss cheese
  (4 ounces)
2 teaspoons all-purpose flour
¼ teaspoon salt
  Dash ground nutmeg
1 cup milk
2 beaten eggs

Prepare Plain Pastry as for a single-crust pie, *except* fit pastry into a 7½-inch quiche dish. Bake at 450° for 5 minutes. Set aside; reduce oven temperature to 325°.

Cook bacon till crisp. Drain; crumble. Reserve 1 tablespoon bacon; sprinkle remaining in pastry shell. Top with cheese. Mix flour, salt, and nutmeg; stir in milk and eggs. Carefully pour over cheese in pastry shell.

Bake, uncovered, at 325° for 30 minutes. Sprinkle with reserved bacon. Bake till knife inserted off-center comes out clean, 5 to 10 minutes more. Let stand 10 minutes before serving. Trim with parsley, if desired. Serves 3 or 4.

Cheese Soufflé (French)

¼ cup butter *or* margarine
¼ cup all-purpose flour
½ teaspoon salt
  Dash cayenne
1 cup milk
8 ounces sharp Cheddar cheese,
  thinly sliced
4 egg whites
4 egg yolks

In saucepan melt butter; blend in flour, salt, and cayenne. Add milk all at once; cook and stir till thickened and bubbly. Remove from heat; stir in cheese till melted.

Beat egg whites till stiff peaks form, about 1½ minutes on medium speed of electric mixer; set aside. In small bowl beat egg yolks till thick and lemon-colored, about 5 minutes on high speed of electric mixer. *Slowly* add cheese mixture, stirring constantly; cool slightly. Gradually pour yolk mixture over beaten egg whites; fold together well. Turn into an ungreased 1½-quart soufflé dish or casserole.

Bake at 300° till knife inserted off-center comes out clean, about 1¼ hours. Serve immediately. Makes 4 servings.

Dilled Lamb Ragout (French)

⅓ cup all-purpose flour
1½ teaspoons salt
½ teaspoon dried dillweed
  Dash pepper
2 pounds boneless lamb, cut
  in ¾-inch cubes
¼ cup cooking oil
1 10-ounce package frozen peas
1 cup sliced celery
½ cup rosé wine
1 cup dairy sour cream

In paper or plastic bag combine flour, salt, dillweed, and pepper. Add lamb cubes, ¼ at a time; shake to coat.

In Dutch oven brown lamb in hot oil. Stir in any flour mixture remaining in bag; blend in 2 cups water. Bake, covered, at 375° for 45 minutes.

Stir in peas, celery, and wine; cover and bake till meat is tender, about 45 minutes longer. Skim off excess fat. Just before serving, stir in sour cream. Heat through *but do not boil.* Makes 6 servings.

Toad in the Hole (British)

2 slices bacon
½ pound fresh pork sausage
  links, cut in ½-inch pieces
1 cup all-purpose flour
1 teaspoon baking powder
1 teaspoon salt
1½ cups milk
3 beaten eggs

Cook bacon till crisp. Drain; set aside 2 tablespoons drippings. Crumble bacon; set aside. In same skillet brown sausage; drain off fat. Stir together flour, baking powder, and salt. Add milk and eggs; beat till smooth.

Spread reserved bacon drippings in a 10x6x2-inch baking dish. Place sausage pieces in dish; sprinkle with crumbled bacon. Pour batter over all. Bake, uncovered, at 400° till set, 30 to 35 minutes. Makes 4 servings.

Steak and Kidney Pie (British)

1 **beef kidney (about 1 pound)**
1 **tablespoon salt**
1 **pound beef round steak, cut in ½-inch cubes**
¼ **cup all-purpose flour**
3 **tablespoons shortening**
1 **medium onion, sliced**
1 **teaspoon Worcestershire sauce**
Plain Pastry (see page 12)
¼ **cup all-purpose flour**
1 **teaspoon salt**
Dash pepper
2 **tablespoons snipped parsley**
Milk

Remove membrane and fat from kidney. Let kidney stand for 1 hour in solution of the 1 tablespoon salt and 4 cups water; drain. Cover with cold water. Bring to boiling; simmer, covered, 20 minutes. Drain; cut into ½-inch cubes. Set aside.

Toss beef with ¼ cup flour. In skillet brown beef in shortening. Add onion, Worcestershire, and 2 cups water. Cover, simmer till meat is tender, about 30 minutes.

Meanwhile, prepare Plain Pastry. Roll out to a circle ½ to 1 inch larger than a 1½-quart casserole; set aside.

Combine ¼ cup flour, the 1 teaspoon salt, and pepper; blend in ½ cup cold water. Stir into hot beef mixture. Cook and stir till slightly thickened and bubbly. Stir in cubed kidney and parsley; heat mixture to boiling.

Pour hot meat mixture into a 1½-quart casserole. Place pastry atop meat mixture. Turn under edges and flute; cut slits for escape of steam. Brush top with milk. Bake, uncovered, at 450° for 20 to 25 minutes. Makes 6 servings.

Cipâte (French-Canadian)

2 **whole large chicken breasts**
1½ **pounds cubed boneless pork, veal, *or* beef**
3 **tablespoons cooking oil**
1 **13¾-ounce can chicken broth**
1 **cup chopped onion**
1 **cup chopped celery**
1 **cup chopped raw potato**
1 **cup sliced carrot**
1 **cup sliced fresh mushrooms**
2 **tablespoons snipped parsley**
1 **teaspoon salt**
⅛ **teaspoon pepper**
⅛ **teaspoon dried savory, crushed**
1 **cup all-purpose flour**
1½ **teaspoons baking powder**
¼ **teaspoon salt**
6 **tablespoons butter**
¼ **cup milk**
2 **tablespoons all-purpose flour**

Remove skin and bones from chicken; cube chicken. In saucepan brown chicken and meat in hot oil. Stir in broth, vegetables, parsley, the 1 teaspoon salt, pepper, and savory. Cook, covered, till meat is tender, 1¼ to 1½ hours.

Meanwhile, to prepare pastry topper stir together the 1 cup flour, baking powder, and the ¼ teaspoon salt. Cut in butter till size of small peas. Add milk; mix well. On lightly floured surface roll out pastry to a circle ½ to 1 inch larger than a 2-quart casserole; set aside.

Blend ⅓ cup cold water into the 2 tablespoons flour. Stir into hot meat mixture. Cook and stir till thickened and bubbly. Turn hot meat mixture into a 2-quart casserole. Place pastry atop meat mixture. Turn under edges and flute; cut slits for escape of steam. Bake, uncovered, at 350° till crust is golden brown, 30 to 35 minutes. Makes 8 to 10 servings.

Tourtière (French-Canadian)

1 **pound lean ground pork**
1 **cup water**
½ **cup finely chopped onion**
½ **cup fine dry bread crumbs**
1 **teaspoon salt**
⅛ **teaspoon ground sage**
Dash pepper
Dash ground nutmeg
2 **recipes Plain Pastry (see page 12)**

In skillet brown ground pork; drain off excess fat. Stir in water, chopped onion, dry bread crumbs, salt, sage, pepper, and nutmeg. Simmer, covered, till onion is tender, about 20 minutes, stirring often.

Meanwhile, prepare Plain Pastry as for a double-crust pie. Fill pastry-lined 9-inch pie plate with hot meat mixture. Adjust top crust; seal and flute edges. Cut slits in top for escape of steam. Bake, uncovered, at 400° till golden brown, about 30 minutes. Cover edges of pastry with foil, if necessary, to prevent overbrowning. Makes 6 servings.

Greek Spinach Pie

½ cup sliced green onion
   with tops
½ teaspoon dried dillweed
1 tablespoon cooking oil
1 10-ounce package frozen
   chopped spinach, thawed
¼ cup butter *or* margarine
¼ cup all-purpose flour
½ teaspoon salt
1½ cups milk
2 beaten eggs
1 cup cream-style cottage cheese
½ cup crumbled feta cheese
   (2 ounces)
¼ teaspoon baking powder
2 16x16-inch sheets fillo dough
2 tablespoons butter, melted

In skillet cook onion and dill in hot oil till onion is tender. Squeeze excess water from spinach; add to skillet. Cook till heated through; keep warm.

In large saucepan melt the ¼ cup butter; blend in flour and salt. Stir in milk all at once. Cook and stir till thickened and bubbly; cook and stir 1 minute more. Stir *half* the hot sauce mixture into eggs; return to saucepan. Stir in cheeses, spinach mixture, and baking powder. Set aside.

Brush *half* of *one* sheet of fillo dough with some of the melted butter; fold in half. Butter half of this dough rectangle and fold again, forming an 8-inch square. Place in greased 8x8x2-inch baking pan. Pour in spinach mixture.

Repeat buttering and folding remaining fillo dough. Place atop spinach mixture; tuck in edges. Bake, uncovered, at 325° till mixture is set and top is browned, 35 to 40 minutes. Let stand 10 minutes. Makes 4 servings.

Pasticchio (Greek)

6 ounces pasticchio macaroni *or*
   elbow macaroni (1½ cups)
⅓ cup grated Parmesan cheese
¼ cup milk
1 beaten egg
¾ pound ground beef
½ cup chopped onion
1 8-ounce can tomato sauce
¾ teaspoon salt
½ teaspoon ground cinnamon
⅛ teaspoon ground nutmeg
⅛ teaspoon pepper
3 tablespoons butter
3 tablespoons all-purpose flour
¼ teaspoon salt
1½ cups milk
1 beaten egg
¼ cup grated Parmesan cheese

Cook macaroni according to package directions; drain. Stir in the ⅓ cup Parmesan, the ¼ cup milk, and 1 egg; set aside.

In skillet cook ground beef and chopped onion till meat is lightly browned and onion is tender; drain off excess fat. Stir in tomato sauce, the ¾ teaspoon salt, the cinnamon, nutmeg, and pepper; set aside.

In saucepan melt butter; blend in flour and the ¼ teaspoon salt. Stir in the 1½ cups milk; cook and stir till thickened and bubbly. Cook and stir 1 minute more. Stir *half* the hot sauce mixture into 1 beaten egg; return all to saucepan. Stir in the ¼ cup Parmesan cheese.

Layer *half* the macaroni mixture in an 8x8x2-inch baking pan. Spoon meat mixture atop, then remaining macaroni. Spread cream sauce over all. Bake, uncovered, at 350° for 45 to 50 minutes. Let stand 10 minutes. Makes 6 servings.

Pasta Pointers

When you cook macaroni, spaghetti, or noodles, use a large pot with plenty of water. (During cooking, macaroni and spaghetti generally double in volume, while the measure of noodles remains about the same.) Add 1 teaspoon of salt for each quart of water and a teaspoon of cooking oil, if desired, to prevent sticking and to prevent boiling over.

Add the pasta to vigorously boiling water, leaving the pan uncovered. Stir a moment to separate pieces. Making sure the water continues to boil, cook without stirring till pasta is barely tender. Drain at once. If you need to hold the pasta before serving, stir in a little butter or oil to keep it from sticking.

Moussaka (Greek)

2 **medium eggplants, peeled and
cut into ½-inch slices
(2 pounds)**
1 **pound ground lamb** *or*
ground beef
1 **cup chopped onion**
¼ **cup dry red wine**
¼ **cup water**
2 **tablespoons snipped parsley**
1 **tablespoon tomato paste**
1 **teaspoon salt**
Dash pepper
¾ **cup soft bread crumbs (1 slice)**
½ **cup shredded sharp American
cheese (2 ounces)**
2 **beaten eggs**
¼ **teaspoon ground cinnamon**
3 **tablespoons butter** *or*
margarine
3 **tablespoons all-purpose flour**
½ **teaspoon salt**
⅛ **teaspoon ground nutmeg**
Dash pepper
1½ **cups milk**
1 **beaten egg**
Cooking oil

Sprinkle eggplant slices with a little salt; set aside. In skillet cook meat and onion till meat is brown; drain off excess fat. Stir in wine, water, parsley, tomato paste, the 1 teaspoon salt, and dash pepper. Simmer till liquid is nearly evaporated, about 4 minutes. Cool slightly.

Stir *half* the bread crumbs, *half* the cheese, the 2 eggs, and cinnamon into meat mixture. Set aside.

In saucepan melt butter; stir in flour, the ½ teaspoon salt, nutmeg, and dash pepper. Add milk all at once; cook and stir till thickened and bubbly. Stir *half* the hot sauce mixture into the 1 beaten egg; return all to saucepan. Cook and stir over low heat 2 minutes. Set aside.

Brown eggplant slices in a little hot oil. Sprinkle bottom of a 12x7½x2-inch baking dish with remaining bread crumbs. Cover with *half* the eggplant.

Spoon meat mixture over eggplant layer. Arrange remaining eggplant atop; pour milk-egg sauce over all. Sprinkle with remaining ¼ cup cheese. Bake, uncovered, at 350° till set, about 45 minutes. Makes 6 to 8 servings.

Paella Casserole (Spanish)

½ **pound chorizos** *or* **Italian
sausage links, sliced**
1 **2½- to 3-pound ready-to-cook
broiler-fryer chicken,
cut up**
1 **medium onion, chopped
(½ cup)**
1 **medium sweet red pepper,
chopped (½ cup)**
1 **medium green pepper, chopped
(½ cup)**
2 **cloves garlic, minced**
1½ **cups regular rice**
2 **medium tomatoes, peeled and
chopped (1½ cups)**
2 **teaspoons salt**
¼ **teaspoon saffron, crushed**
4 **cups boiling water**
1 **pound fresh** *or* **frozen shelled
shrimp**
10 **small clams in shells**
1 **10-ounce package frozen peas**

In large skillet cook sausage over medium heat till done. Drain sausage, reserving drippings in skillet; set aside.

Season chicken pieces with a little salt and pepper. Brown chicken in reserved drippings; remove chicken, reserving drippings in skillet.

Add chopped onion, red pepper, green pepper, and garlic to reserved drippings; cook till onion is tender but not brown. Stir in uncooked rice, chopped tomatoes, salt, and saffron. Stir in boiling water; bring mixture to boiling. Stir in cooked sausage.

Turn rice mixture into a paella pan *or* a 4-quart casserole *or* a Dutch oven; arrange chicken pieces atop mixture. Bake, covered, at 375° for 30 minutes.

Meanwhile, thaw frozen shrimp. Thoroughly scrub clams. Place clams in a saucepan with ½ inch of boiling water; cover and cook till shells open, 3 to 5 minutes. Drain; discard any clams that do not open.

Place peas in a colander or strainer; rinse with hot water to thaw. Arrange peas, clams, and shrimp atop rice mixture. Bake, covered, till chicken and rice are done, 15 to 20 minutes longer. Garnish with lemon slices, if desired. Serves 8.

Paella Casserole, a Spanish specialty, offers a festival of flavors in a single
dish. This colorful entrée includes sausage, chicken, shrimp, clams, peas, and saffron rice.

Chicken Enchiladas (Mexican)

1 **cup chopped onion**
1 **clove garlic, minced**
2 **tablespoons cooking oil**
1 **tablespoon all-purpose flour**
1 **16-ounce can tomatoes, cut up**
1 **15-ounce can tomato sauce**
1 **4-ounce can green chili peppers, drained, seeded, and chopped**
1 **teaspoon sugar**
1 **teaspoon ground cumin**
¼ **teaspoon salt**
2 **cups chopped cooked chicken**
1½ **cups shredded sharp American cheese (6 ounces)**
¼ **cup finely chopped onion**
¼ **cup chopped pitted ripe olives**
¾ **teaspoon salt**
12 **frozen corn tortillas, thawed**
Cooking oil
¼ **cup sliced pitted ripe olives**

Cook the 1 cup chopped onion and garlic in the 2 tablespoons oil till onion is tender but not brown; stir in flour. Add undrained tomatoes, tomato sauce, chili peppers, sugar, cumin, and the ¼ teaspoon salt. Cook and stir till thickened and bubbly; set aside.

Combine chicken, *half* the cheese, the ¼ cup onion, the chopped olives, and the ¾ teaspoon salt. Set aside.

In skillet dip tortillas briefly in small amount of hot oil till limp but not crisp; drain. Spoon ¼ *cup* of the chicken mixture onto each tortilla; roll up.

Place filled tortillas in a 13x9x2-inch baking dish. Pour tomato mixture over all. Bake, covered, at 350° about 15 minutes. Uncover; bake till heated through, about 15 minutes more. Sprinkle with remaining shredded cheese; return to oven till cheese melts, 2 or 3 minutes. Top with the sliced olives. Makes 6 servings.

Brunch Eggs Ranchero (Mexican)

5 **slices bacon, cut up**
1 **16-ounce can tomatoes, cut up**
2 **tablespoons chopped canned green chili peppers (about 2 peppers)**
1 **clove garlic, minced**
4 **eggs**
Salt
Pepper
4 **slices bacon**

In skillet cook the cut-up bacon slices till crisp; drain off fat. Stir in undrained tomatoes, chili peppers, and garlic; heat through. Divide among 4 individual casseroles.

Carefully break one egg atop tomato mixture in *each* casserole. Season eggs lightly with salt and pepper. Bake, uncovered, at 325° till eggs are set, 20 to 25 minutes.

Cook the 4 bacon slices till done *but not crisp;* drain. Insert tines of fork into one end of each bacon slice; turn fork to wind bacon around it. Remove fork. Garnish each casserole with a bacon curl. Makes 4 servings.

Pastel de Chocolo (South American)

2 **tablespoons raisins**
1 **pound ground beef**
2 **cups chopped onion**
½ **small clove garlic, minced**
1 **tablespoon ground cumin**
1½ **teaspoons paprika**
1 **teaspoon salt**
⅛ **teaspoon pepper**
½ **cup chopped pitted ripe olives**
1 **2½- to 3-pound ready-to-cook broiler-fryer chicken, cut up**
2 **tablespoons olive oil**
1 **10-ounce package frozen corn**
1 **cup dry white wine**

Soak raisins in ¼ cup hot water till plump; set aside. Cook beef, onion, and garlic till meat is brown and onion is tender; drain off fat. Stir in raisins with their liquid, cumin, paprika, salt, and pepper; turn into a 3-quart casserole. Spread chopped olives evenly over meat mixture; set aside.

Brown chicken lightly in the olive oil about 15 minutes. Arrange chicken atop meat mixture. Top with corn; season with more salt and pepper. Pour wine over all.

Bake, covered, at 350° for 45 minutes. Spread corn evenly over casserole, if necessary. Bake, uncovered, 15 minutes more. Serve over hot cooked rice, if desired. Makes 8 servings.

Veal Parmesan Casserole (Italian)

6 ounces spaghetti
1½ pounds boneless veal round
    or sirloin steak, cut in
    6 serving-size pieces
¼ cup all-purpose flour
½ teaspoon salt
    Dash pepper
1 beaten egg
2 tablespoons milk
⅓ cup fine dry bread crumbs
⅓ cup grated Parmesan cheese
3 tablespoons cooking oil
1 large green pepper,
    finely chopped
    (1 cup)
1 large onion, finely chopped
    (1 cup)
2 cloves garlic, minced
2 15-ounce cans tomato sauce
¼ cup water
1 teaspoon dried basil,
    crushed
1 cup shredded mozzarella
    cheese (4 ounces)
¼ cup grated Parmesan cheese

Break spaghetti pieces in half. Cook spaghetti according to package directions; drain and set aside. Pound veal pieces to ¼-inch thickness.

In shallow dish combine flour, salt, and pepper. In another dish combine egg and milk; in a third dish mix crumbs and the ⅓ cup Parmesan. Coat veal with flour mixture; dip in egg mixture, then in crumbs. In large skillet brown meat on both sides in hot oil, 2 or 3 pieces at a time; remove meat, reserving drippings in skillet.

In reserved drippings cook green pepper, onion, and garlic till onion is tender. Stir in tomato sauce, water, and basil. Set aside ½ *cup* of the sauce; stir remaining sauce into cooked spaghetti. Turn spaghetti mixture into a 13x9x2-inch baking dish; arrange veal atop.

Spoon reserved sauce over meat. Bake, covered, at 350° for 40 minutes. Sprinkle with mozzarella and the ¼ cup Parmesan. Bake, uncovered, 10 minutes more. Makes 6 servings.

Pizza Siciliana (pictured on page 5)

4½ cups all-purpose flour
1 package active dry yeast
1½ teaspoons salt
1½ cups *warm* water (110°)
2 tablespoons cooking oil
1 cup chopped onion
1 clove garlic, minced
2 tablespoons olive oil
1 16-ounce can tomatoes,
    cut up
1 6-ounce can tomato paste
1½ teaspoons dried basil,
    crushed
1½ teaspoons dried oregano,
    crushed
1 teaspoon salt
½ teaspoon sugar
⅛ teaspoon pepper
½ cup chopped onion
½ cup sliced pitted
    ripe olives
1 medium green pepper,
    cut in strips
2 cups shredded mozzarella
    cheese (8 ounces)
¼ cup grated Parmesan cheese

Combine *2 cups* of the flour, yeast, and the 1½ teaspoons salt. Add water and cooking oil. Beat at low speed of electric mixer for ½ minute, scraping bowl. Beat 3 minutes at high speed. By hand, stir in enough of the remaining flour to make moderately stiff dough. On floured surface, knead till smooth. Place in greased bowl; turn once. Cover; let rise till double (about 1 hour).

Cook the 1 cup chopped onion and garlic in olive oil till onion is tender. Add undrained tomatoes, tomato paste, basil, oregano, salt, sugar, and pepper. Bring mixture to boiling; cover and simmer for 10 minutes.

Pat dough from center to edges in a greased 15½x10½x1-inch baking pan. Cover; let rise 45 minutes. Spoon sauce over dough. Bake, uncovered, at 475° for 25 minutes.

Sprinkle pizza with the ½ cup onion and olives. Top with green pepper; sprinkle mozzarella and Parmesan cheese over. Bake 10 to 15 minutes longer. Makes 6 servings.

5 Rounding Out the Meal

Have you ever wondered what to serve with a roast without spending the whole afternoon in the kitchen? . . . how to get the family to eat vegetables? . . . where to find a dessert that even your mother-in-law will like? This chapter is full of delicious answers—side dishes that cook without supervision, recipes that make vegetables fun to eat, and oven desserts with universal appeal.

Bake colorful vegetable and dessert casseroles along with a roast or meat loaf.
For variety, try *Corn-Zucchini Bake, Carrot-Rice Bake,* and *Peach-Pecan Dessert* (see page 90).

Vegetable Favorites

Corn-Zucchini Bake

1 **pound zucchini (3 medium)**
¼ **cup chopped onion**
1 **tablespoon butter** *or* **margarine**
1 **10-ounce package frozen whole kernel corn, cooked and drained,** *or* **2 cups fresh corn cut from cob, cooked and drained**
1 **cup shredded Swiss cheese (4 ounces)**
2 **beaten eggs**
¼ **teaspoon salt**
¼ **cup fine dry bread crumbs**
2 **tablespoons grated Parmesan cheese**
1 **tablespoon butter** *or* **margarine, melted**

Wash zucchini; do not peel. Cut into 1-inch-thick slices. Cook, covered, in a small amount of boiling salted water till tender, 15 to 20 minutes. Drain and mash with fork.

Cook onion in 1 tablespoon butter till tender. Combine zucchini, onion, cooked corn, Swiss cheese, eggs, and salt. Turn mixture into a 1-quart casserole.

Combine crumbs, Parmesan, and melted butter; sprinkle over corn mixture. Place casserole on a baking sheet. Bake, uncovered, at 350° till knife inserted off-center comes out clean, about 40 minutes.

Let stand 5 to 10 minutes before serving. Garnish with cherry tomatoes and parsley, if desired. Makes 6 servings.

Carrot-Rice Bake

4 **cups water**
1 **tablespoon instant chicken bouillon granules**
1 **teaspoon salt**
2 **cups chopped carrot**
1½ **cups regular rice**
2 **tablespoons butter** *or* **margarine**
½ **teaspoon dried thyme, crushed**
½ **cup shredded sharp American cheese (2 ounces)**

In saucepan bring water, bouillon granules, and salt to boiling. Stir in carrot, rice, butter, and thyme; return to boiling. Turn mixture into a 2-quart casserole.

Bake, covered, at 325° for 25 minutes; stir. Sprinkle with cheese. Bake, uncovered, about 5 minutes longer. Garnish with parsley, if desired. Makes 8 servings.

Spiced Beets with Apples

½ **cup chopped onion**
2 **tablespoons butter** *or* **margarine**
1 **large apple, peeled, cored, and sliced (1¼ cups)**
2 **tablespoons brown sugar**
½ **teaspoon ground allspice**
¼ **teaspoon salt**
1 **16-ounce can diced beets, drained**
2 **tablespoons chopped walnuts (optional)**

In saucepan cook onion, covered, in butter till nearly tender, about 4 minutes. Add apple; cook, covered, till tender, 3 to 4 minutes, stirring once or twice. Remove from heat. Stir brown sugar, allspice, and salt into apple mixture; fold in beets. Turn into a 1-quart casserole. Bake, uncovered, at 350° till hot, 25 to 30 minutes. Stir before serving; sprinkle with nuts, if desired. Serves 4 to 6.

Microwave cooking directions: Place onion and butter in a 1-quart nonmetal casserole. Cook, covered, in countertop microwave oven till onion is nearly tender, about 2 minutes. Add apple slices. Cover; micro-cook till tender, 2 to 3 minutes. Stir brown sugar, allspice, and salt into apple mixture; fold in beets. Micro-cook, uncovered, till hot, about 6 minutes, stirring after 3 minutes. Stir again before serving; sprinkle with nuts, if desired.

Mexicali Bean Bake

½ **cup chopped onion**
1 **clove garlic, minced**
6 **tablespoons cooking oil**
1 **tablespoon all-purpose flour**
2 **15½-ounce cans red kidney beans, drained**
1 **16-ounce can tomatoes, cut up**
1 **4-ounce can mild green chili peppers, drained, seeded, and chopped**
  Several dashes bottled hot pepper sauce
⅔ **cup yellow cornmeal**
¾ **teaspoon salt**
¼ **teaspoon baking soda**
½ **cup milk**
1 **beaten egg**
1 **12-ounce can whole kernel corn with sweet peppers, drained**
1 **cup shredded American cheese**

In large saucepan cook onion and garlic in *2 tablespoons* of the oil till onion is tender but not brown; blend in flour. Stir in beans, undrained tomatoes, chili peppers, and hot pepper sauce. Cook and stir till slightly thickened and bubbly. Remove from heat and set aside.

In bowl mix cornmeal, salt, and soda. Combine milk, egg, and remaining 4 tablespoons oil. Add to dry ingredients along with corn; mix well. (Mixture will be thin.)

Pour *about ⅔* of the cornmeal mixture into a greased 2-quart casserole or a 12x7½x2-inch baking dish. Sprinkle with cheese; spoon bean mixture over all. Spoon remaining cornmeal mixture around edge of casserole. Bake, uncovered, at 350° till corn bread topper is done, about 35 minutes. Makes 8 to 10 servings.

Saucy Celery Casserole

4 **cups thinly sliced celery**
¼ **cup butter *or* margarine**
2 **tablespoons all-purpose flour**
¼ **teaspoon salt**
1 **cup milk**
1 **cup shredded sharp American cheese (4 ounces)**
1 **4-ounce can chopped mushrooms, drained**
2 **tablespoons chopped green pepper**
2 **tablespoons chopped pimiento**

Cook celery, covered, in butter till crisp-tender, about 15 minutes; stir in flour and salt. Add milk; cook and stir till thickened and bubbly. Add ¾ cup of the cheese; stir till melted. Stir in mushrooms, pepper, and pimiento. Turn into a 1-quart casserole. Bake, uncovered, at 350° for 20 minutes. Sprinkle with remaining ¼ cup cheese. Serves 6.

Microwave cooking directions: In 1-quart nonmetal casserole cook celery in butter, covered, in countertop microwave oven till crisp-tender, 6 to 7 minutes; stir after 3 minutes. Stir in flour and salt. Add milk, ¾ cup of the cheese, mushrooms, pepper, and pimiento; mix well. Micro-cook, uncovered, till thickened and bubbly, 4 to 5 minutes, stirring after every minute. Sprinkle with remaining ¼ cup cheese.

Golden Crumb Broccoli

1½ **pounds fresh broccoli**
1 **10¾-ounce can condensed cream of mushroom soup**
¼ **cup mayonnaise**
¼ **cup shredded sharp American cheese (1 ounce)**
1 **tablespoon chopped pimiento**
1½ **teaspoons lemon juice**
⅓ **cup crushed round cheese crackers (8 crackers)**

Cut up broccoli to make about 6 cups. In saucepan cook broccoli, covered, in small amount of boiling salted water for 10 to 15 minutes; drain well. Turn into a 1½-quart casserole. Mix soup, mayonnaise, cheese, pimiento, and lemon juice. Pour over broccoli. Top with crushed crackers. Bake, uncovered, at 350° for 35 minutes. Makes 6 to 8 servings.

All vegetable casseroles are not alike. *Mexicali Bean Bake* boasts a hot, spicy flavor;
Saucy Celery Casserole has a fresh, light taste; and *Golden Crumb Broccoli* is rich and creamy.

Casserole vegetables such as onion-crowned *Easy Vegetable Bake* and crumb-topped *Scalloped Succotash* are perfect for serving at a buffet or toting to your next church supper.

Easy Vegetable Bake

1   **1¼-ounce envelope sour cream sauce mix**
1   **10-ounce package frozen Parisian-style vegetables with sauce**
1   **1½-ounce envelope white sauce mix**
¼   **teaspoon salt**
1   **cup milk**
3   **cups frozen Southern-style hash brown potatoes, thawed**
½   **of a 3-ounce can French-fried onions**

Prepare sour cream sauce mix according to package directions; set aside. In large saucepan cook frozen Parisian-style vegetables according to package directions; do not drain. Stir in dry white sauce mix and salt; gradually stir in milk. Bring to boiling, stirring constantly. Stir in sour cream sauce and hash browns.

Turn vegetable mixture into a 12x7½x2-inch baking dish. Bake, uncovered, at 350° till hot, about 30 minutes. Circle edge of casserole with French-fried onions. Bake 5 minutes more. Trim with parsley, if desired. Makes 10 servings.

Scalloped Succotash

2 17-ounce cans whole kernel
   corn
1 16-ounce can lima beans,
   drained
1 13-ounce can evaporated milk
1 cup shredded Swiss cheese
   (4 ounces)
2 beaten eggs
¼ cup sliced green onion
   with tops
¼ cup chopped pimiento
   Dash pepper
2 cups coarsely crushed saltine
   crackers (44 crackers)
2 tablespoons butter, melted

Drain corn, reserving liquid. Add water to corn liquid, if necessary, to make ¾ cup. In bowl combine corn liquid, corn, limas, evaporated milk, cheese, eggs, onion, pimiento, pepper, and *1½ cups* of the cracker crumbs. Turn into a 2½-quart casserole. Bake, covered, at 350° for 30 minutes.

Toss together the remaining ½ cup cracker crumbs and melted butter to combine; sprinkle atop casserole. Bake, uncovered, 45 to 50 minutes more. Let stand 10 minutes before serving. Garnish with a parsley sprig and halved cherry tomato, if desired. Makes 12 servings.

Crowd-Pleasing Vegetable Bake

1 20-ounce package frozen
   cauliflower
1 10-ounce package frozen cut
   broccoli
1 17-ounce can cream-style corn
1 17-ounce can whole kernel corn,
   drained
2 cups shredded Swiss cheese
   (8 ounces)
1 10¾-ounce can condensed
   cream of celery soup
1 4-ounce can sliced mushrooms,
   drained
1½ cups soft rye bread crumbs
   (2 slices)
2 tablespoons butter, melted

Cook cauliflower and broccoli according to package directions; drain. Cut up any large pieces.

Combine cream-style corn, drained whole kernel corn, cheese, and soup. Fold in cooked vegetables and mushrooms. Turn mixture into a 13x9x2-inch baking dish.

Toss bread crumbs with melted butter; sprinkle atop casserole. Bake, uncovered, at 375° for 30 to 35 minutes. Let stand 10 minutes before serving. Makes 10 to 12 servings.

Pea and Celery Bake

1 10-ounce package frozen peas
1 bunch celery, bias-cut in
   1-inch pieces (4½ cups)
½ cup chopped onion
2 teaspoons instant chicken
   bouillon granules
1 8-ounce can tomato sauce
2 tablespoons butter
½ teaspoon dried oregano,
   crushed
⅓ cup grated Parmesan cheese

In colander or strainer rinse peas with hot water to thaw. In saucepan mix celery, onion, bouillon granules, and ½ cup water. Cover; bring to boiling. Reduce heat and simmer till celery is tender, 12 to 15 minutes. Stir in peas, tomato sauce, butter, and oregano.

Turn mixture into a 1½-quart casserole. Bake, uncovered, at 400° till done, about 30 minutes. Sprinkle with cheese. Makes 6 to 8 servings.

Scalloped Tomatoes

½ **cup chopped onion**
¼ **cup butter** *or* **margarine**
3 **slices bread, coarsely crumbled (2¼ cups)**
6 **medium tomatoes, peeled and sliced (about 3½ cups)**
  Salt
  Pepper
  Sugar

Cook onion in butter till tender but not brown; stir in bread crumbs. In a 1-quart casserole layer *half* the tomatoes; sprinkle with salt, pepper, and sugar. Cover with *half* the crumb mixture. Repeat layers. Bake, uncovered, at 350° for 30 minutes. Makes 6 servings.

Microwave cooking directions: Place onion and butter in a glass bowl. Cook, uncovered, in a countertop microwave oven till onion is tender, 2 to 3 minutes; stir in bread.

In a 1-quart casserole layer *half* the tomatoes; sprinkle with salt, pepper, and sugar. Cover with *half* the crumb mixture. Repeat layers. Micro-cook, uncovered, 9 to 10 minutes; give dish a half turn after 5 minutes.

Asparagus-Egg Casserole (pictured on page 4)

½ **cup chopped celery**
¼ **cup butter** *or* **margarine**
¼ **cup all-purpose flour**
½ **teaspoon salt**
½ **teaspoon dry mustard**
  Dash pepper
1¾ **cups milk**
1 **teaspoon instant chicken bouillon granules**
1 **4-ounce can chopped mushrooms, drained**
2 **8-ounce packages frozen cut asparagus**
3 **hard-cooked eggs, sliced**
½ **cup crushed rich round crackers (12 crackers)**

In saucepan cook celery in butter; blend in flour, salt, mustard, and pepper. Add milk and bouillon granules. Cook and stir till thickened and bubbly. Stir in mushrooms; set aside. Cook the frozen asparagus according to package directions; drain thoroughly.

Reserve ½ cup asparagus and 1 egg for garnish. In a 10x6x2-inch baking dish arrange remaining asparagus and egg slices. Pour sauce over all. Bake, covered, at 375° for 15 minutes. Arrange reserved asparagus and sliced egg atop casserole; sprinkle with crushed crackers. Bake, uncovered, 10 minutes longer. Makes 6 servings.

Artichokes with Fresh Mushrooms

3 **cups fresh mushrooms, halved**
½ **cup sliced green onion with tops**
¼ **cup butter** *or* **margarine**
2 **tablespoons all-purpose flour**
⅛ **teaspoon salt**
  Dash pepper
¾ **cup water**
¼ **cup milk**
1 **teaspoon instant chicken bouillon granules**
1 **teaspoon lemon juice**
⅛ **teaspoon ground nutmeg**
1 **9-ounce package frozen artichoke hearts, cooked and drained**
¾ **cup soft bread crumbs (1 slice)**
1 **tablespoon butter** *or* **margarine, melted**

Cook mushroom halves and sliced green onion in the ¼ cup butter or margarine. With slotted spoon remove vegetables and set aside, reserving pan drippings.

Blend flour, salt, and pepper into reserved pan drippings. Stir in water, milk, bouillon granules, lemon juice, and nutmeg. Cook and stir till thickened and bubbly. Stir in mushroom mixture and cooked artichoke hearts.

Turn mixture into a 1-quart casserole. Combine bread crumbs and the melted butter; sprinkle around edge. Bake, uncovered, at 350° for 20 minutes. Makes 6 servings.

Spinach-Cheese Casserole

2 slices bacon
½ cup chopped carrot
¼ cup chopped onion
1 11-ounce can condensed
  Cheddar cheese soup
2 10-ounce packages frozen
  chopped spinach,
  thawed and drained
1 cup cooked rice
¼ cup milk

In a 2-quart saucepan cook bacon till crisp; drain, reserving drippings. Crumble bacon and set aside. In reserved drippings cook carrot and onion till onion is tender. Stir in soup, spinach, rice, and milk.

Turn mixture into a 1-quart casserole. Bake, covered, at 375° till heated through, 35 to 40 minutes. Sprinkle with the crumbled bacon. Makes 6 to 8 servings.

Onion-Hominy Bake

1 14½-ounce can golden hominy
1 3-ounce can French-fried
  onions
1 15½-ounce can cut green beans,
  drained
1 10¾-ounce can condensed
  cream of mushroom soup
½ cup shredded sharp American
  cheese (2 ounces)
1 teaspoon Worcestershire sauce

Drain hominy, reserving ¼ cup of the liquid. Chop *half* the French-fried onions. Combine hominy, reserved liquid, chopped onions, green beans, soup, cheese, and Worcestershire.

Turn into a 1½-quart casserole. Bake, covered, at 375° for 25 to 30 minutes. Uncover; top with remaining onions. Bake, uncovered, 5 minutes more. Makes 6 to 8 servings.

Casserole Carrots

2 pounds carrots
2 tablespoons butter *or*
  margarine
2 tablespoons all-purpose flour
¾ teaspoon dry mustard
½ teaspoon salt
¼ teaspoon paprika
⅛ teaspoon pepper
2 cups milk
¼ cup grated Parmesan cheese
½ cup canned French-fried onions

Peel carrots; slice crosswise on the bias. Cook, covered, in boiling salted water till just tender, about 20 minutes; drain thoroughly. Set aside.

In a small saucepan melt butter; blend in flour, dry mustard, salt, paprika, and pepper. Add milk all at once. Cook and stir till thickened and bubbly. Stir in cheese.

Combine cooked carrots and sauce; turn into a 1½-quart casserole. Bake, covered, at 350° for 30 minutes. Uncover; sprinkle French-fried onions over casserole. Bake, uncovered, 3 to 5 minutes more. Makes 8 servings.

Caraway-Sour Cream Cabbage

½ cup water
½ teaspoon salt
6 cups shredded cabbage
1 large onion, sliced (1 cup)
1 cup dairy sour cream
2 tablespoons all-purpose flour
1 tablespoon prepared mustard
1 teaspoon caraway seed
½ teaspoon salt
⅛ teaspoon pepper
  Paprika

In saucepan bring the water and ½ teaspoon salt to boiling. Add cabbage and onion; cook, covered, till crisp-tender, 7 to 8 minutes. Drain, reserving cooking liquid. Add enough water to cooking liquid to make ¾ cup.

In same saucepan blend together sour cream, flour, mustard, caraway seed, ½ teaspoon salt, and pepper. Stir in cooking liquid. Fold in cabbage and onion.

Turn mixture into a 1½-quart casserole. Bake, covered, at 350° till heated through, about 20 minutes, stirring once. Sprinkle generously with paprika. Makes 6 servings.

Cheddar-Squash Bake

2 pounds yellow crookneck
   summer squash *or* zucchini
1 cup dairy sour cream
2 beaten egg yolks
2 tablespoons all-purpose flour
2 stiffly beaten egg whites
1½ cups shredded Cheddar cheese
4 slices bacon, crisp-cooked,
   drained, and crumbled
⅓ cup fine dry bread crumbs
1 tablespoon butter, melted

Scrub squash; cut off ends. Do not peel. Slice to make 6 cups. Cook, covered, in small amount of boiling salted water till tender, 15 to 20 minutes. Drain well; sprinkle with salt. Reserve a few slices squash for garnish.

Mix sour cream, egg yolks, and flour; fold in egg whites. In a 12x7½x2-inch baking dish layer *half* the squash, *half* the egg mixture, and *half* the cheese; sprinkle bacon atop. Repeat layers of squash, egg, and cheese.

Combine crumbs and butter; sprinkle atop. Arrange reserved squash atop. Bake, uncovered, at 350° for 20 to 25 minutes. Top with bacon and parsley, if desired. Serves 8 to 10.

Turnip Puff

1 pound turnips (4 medium)
2 tablespoons butter
2 beaten eggs
¾ cup soft bread crumbs (1 slice)
1 tablespoon finely chopped
   onion
1 tablespoon snipped parsley
1 tablespoon sugar
1 teaspoon salt
1 teaspoon lemon juice

Peel and cube turnips to make about 3 cups. Cook, covered, in small amount of boiling salted water till tender, about 20 minutes; drain. Add butter and mash.

In bowl combine eggs, bread crumbs, onion, parsley, sugar, salt, and lemon juice. Add mashed turnips; mix well. Turn mixture into a 3-cup casserole. Bake, uncovered, at 375° till set, 25 to 30 minutes. Garnish with more parsley, if desired. Makes 4 servings.

Broccoli-Stuffing Bake

2 cups milk
1 cup shredded sharp American
   cheese (4 ounces)
4 beaten eggs
3 cups herb-seasoned stuffing
   croutons
1 10-ounce package frozen
   chopped broccoli, thawed

In a saucepan heat and stir together milk and cheese till blended; remove from heat. In a mixing bowl gradually stir hot mixture into eggs. Add stuffing croutons, broccoli, and ¼ teaspoon salt; mix well.

Turn mixture into a greased 1½-quart casserole. Bake, uncovered, at 325° for 45 minutes. Makes 6 to 8 servings.

Scalloped Zucchini

6 medium zucchini (2 pounds)
¼ pound bulk pork sausage
¼ cup chopped onion
½ cup grated Parmesan cheese
½ cup finely crushed saltine
   crackers (14 crackers)
2 beaten eggs
1 teaspoon salt
⅛ teaspoon dried thyme, crushed

Scrub squash; cut off ends. Do not peel. Cook, covered, in boiling salted water till tender, about 15 minutes. Drain well, reserving ½ cup liquid. Chop zucchini.

Cook sausage and onion till sausage is brown; drain off fat. Reserve 2 *tablespoons* of the Parmesan. Add remaining Parmesan, squash, reserved liquid, crackers, eggs, salt, and thyme to sausage; mix well. Turn into a 1½-quart casserole; sprinkle with reserved Parmesan. Bake, uncovered, at 350° till set, 40 to 45 minutes. Makes 8 servings.

Celebrate a big squash
crop with *Cheddar-Squash Bake.*
This golden casserole is
layered with yellow crookneck
squash, Cheddar cheese,
sour cream, and crumbled bacon.

Light and fluffy *Turnip
Puff* is accented with parsley,
lemon juice, and onion.
Easy to make, this casserole
turns the everyday turnip
into an extra-special treat.

Green Beans Parmesan (pictured on the cover)

2 9-ounce packages frozen
  French-style green beans
  Milk
¼ cup chopped onion
2 tablespoons butter *or*
  margarine
2 tablespoons all-purpose flour
½ teaspoon salt
¼ cup grated Parmesan cheese
1 5-ounce can water chestnuts,
  drained and sliced
¾ cup soft bread crumbs
2 tablespoons butter, melted

Cook beans according to package directions; drain, reserving liquid. Add milk to reserved liquid to make 1¼ cups; set aside. In saucepan cook onion in 2 tablespoons butter till tender; blend in flour and salt. Stir in milk mixture all at once; cook and stir till thickened and bubbly. Stir in *half* the Parmesan cheese. Stir in the cooked beans and sliced water chestnuts; turn into a 1-quart casserole.

Toss crumbs with remaining Parmesan and melted butter to combine; sprinkle atop casserole. Bake, uncovered, at 350° till bubbly, about 30 minutes. Garnish with additional sliced water chestnuts, if desired. Makes 6 to 8 servings.

Onion-Cauliflower Bake

1 10-ounce package frozen
  cauliflower, thawed
2 9-ounce packages frozen
  onions with cream sauce
1½ cups water
2 tablespoons butter
¾ cup shredded sharp American
  cheese (3 ounces)
¼ cup toasted slivered almonds
1 tablespoon snipped parsley
½ cup canned French-fried
  onions, crumbled

Cut up any large pieces of cauliflower; set aside. In a saucepan combine frozen onions, water, and butter. Cover; bring to boiling. Reduce heat and simmer for 4 minutes, stirring occasionally. Remove from heat; stir till sauce is smooth. Stir in cauliflower, cheese, almonds, and parsley. Turn mixture into a 1½-quart casserole.

Bake, uncovered, at 350° till bubbly, about 35 minutes. Top with crumbled French-fried onions; bake, uncovered, 5 minutes longer. Makes 8 servings.

Cheesy Lima Casserole

1 cup large dry lima beans
2½ cups water
½ cup shredded American cheese
⅓ cup chopped onion
½ teaspoon salt
¼ teaspoon ground sage
  Dash pepper
3 slices bacon, crisp-cooked,
  drained, and crumbled

Rinse beans; place in saucepan. Add water; soak overnight. (Or, bring to boiling; cover and simmer 2 minutes. Let stand 1 hour.) Do not drain. Simmer, covered, for 1 hour. Add cheese, onion, salt, sage, and pepper; mix well.

Turn mixture into a 1-quart casserole. Bake, uncovered, at 350° for 35 minutes. Sprinkle with crumbled bacon just before serving. Makes 3 or 4 servings.

Maple-Baked Beans

1½ pounds dry navy beans
12 cups water
4 ounces salt pork, cubed
½ cup chopped onion
½ cup packed brown sugar
½ cup maple-flavored syrup
1 teaspoon salt
1 teaspoon dry mustard

Rinse beans; place in kettle. Add water; soak overnight. (Or, bring to boiling; cover and simmer 2 minutes. Let stand 1 hour.) Bring water and beans to boiling; simmer till tender, about 40 minutes. Drain; reserve liquid.

In a 3-quart casserole combine beans, pork, onion, sugar, syrup, salt, mustard, and *1½ cups* of the reserved liquid. Bake, covered, at 300° till beans are done, 3½ to 4 hours. Stir occasionally; add more bean liquid, if needed. Serves 8.

Corn-Mushroom Bake

¼ cup all-purpose flour
1 17-ounce can cream-style corn
1 3-ounce package cream cheese,
   cut in cubes
½ teaspoon onion salt
1 17-ounce can whole kernel corn,
   drained
1 4-ounce can sliced mushrooms,
   drained
½ cup shredded Swiss cheese
1½ cups soft bread crumbs
3 tablespoons butter, melted

In saucepan stir flour into cream-style corn. Add cream cheese and onion salt; heat and stir till cream cheese melts. Stir in whole kernel corn, sliced mushrooms, and shredded Swiss cheese.

Turn mixture into a 1½-quart casserole. Toss crumbs with melted butter to combine; sprinkle atop casserole. Bake, uncovered, at 400° till heated through, 30 to 40 minutes. Makes 6 to 8 servings.

Creamed Potatoes Supreme

4 medium potatoes, peeled and
   thinly sliced (4 cups)
1 cup sliced leeks
1 teaspoon salt
1 cup whipping cream
2 tablespoons butter or
   margarine
1 cup shredded Swiss cheese
   (4 ounces)

Combine potatoes, leeks, and salt in a 1½-quart casserole. Add whipping cream; dot with butter. Bake, covered, at 350° till potatoes are tender, about 1 hour. Sprinkle with shredded cheese; bake till cheese melts, about 3 minutes longer. Makes 6 servings.

Cheese-Potato Scallop

4 medium potatoes, peeled and
   thinly sliced
½ cup chopped onion
1 4-ounce can chopped
   mushrooms, drained
1 11-ounce can condensed
   Cheddar cheese soup
1 8-ounce can tomatoes, cut up
1 cup herb-seasoned stuffing
   croutons

In a 10x6x2-inch baking dish layer *half* the potatoes, *half* the onion, and *half* the mushrooms. Season with a little salt. In bowl combine cheese soup and undrained tomatoes; pour *half* the soup mixture over vegetables in baking dish. Repeat layers, ending with soup.

Bake, covered, at 350° for 1½ to 1¾ hours. Uncover; top with croutons. Bake, uncovered, 5 minutes more. Let stand 10 to 15 minutes. Makes 8 servings.

Wild Rice Casserole

1 cup wild rice
2¼ cups chicken broth
2 cups chopped celery
¾ cup chopped onion
¼ cup butter or margarine
1 8-ounce can sliced mushrooms,
   drained
1 tablespoon dried parsley
   flakes
½ teaspoon salt
¼ teaspoon dried thyme, crushed

Rinse rice according to package directions. In a 2-quart saucepan combine rice and chicken broth; bring to boiling. Cover; reduce heat and simmer 40 minutes. Do not drain.

Meanwhile, cook celery and onion in butter till tender but not brown. Stir in mushrooms, parsley flakes, salt, and thyme; stir into rice. Turn into a 1½-quart casserole. Bake, covered, at 325° for 35 to 40 minutes. Stir before serving. Makes 10 to 12 servings.

Dessert Specials

Cheese-Baked Apples

3 tablespoons granulated sugar
2 tablespoons brown sugar
2 tablespoons all-purpose flour
¾ teaspoon ground cinnamon
¼ teaspoon salt
⅓ cup water
1 tablespoon lemon juice
6 medium baking apples, peeled, cored, and cut into eighths
½ cup shredded Cheddar cheese (2 ounces)

In mixing bowl combine sugars, flour, cinnamon, and salt; stir in water and lemon juice. Add apples; stir to coat.

Arrange apples in a 9-inch pie plate; drizzle sugar mixture over all. Bake, covered, at 350° till apples are tender, 45 to 50 minutes. Uncover; sprinkle with cheese. Bake, uncovered, 5 minutes more. Makes 6 servings.

Cranberry-Peach Cobbler

Cobbler Topper (see below)
½ cup sugar
1 tablespoon cornstarch
1 cup cranberry juice cocktail
3 cups sliced peeled fresh *or* frozen peaches (6 medium)
½ cup fresh *or* frozen cranberries

Prepare Cobbler Topper; set aside. In saucepan combine sugar and cornstarch. Stir in juice; cook and stir till thickened and bubbly. Stir in peaches and cranberries. Cook, uncovered, till cranberry skins pop, about 5 minutes.

Turn into a 1½-quart casserole. Immediately spoon topper in 8 mounds atop *hot* fruit. Bake, uncovered, at 400° for 20 to 25 minutes. Serve warm with vanilla ice cream, if desired. Makes 8 servings.

Cobbler Topper

1 cup all-purpose flour
2 tablespoons sugar
1½ teaspoons baking powder
¼ teaspoon salt
¼ cup butter *or* margarine
1 beaten egg
¼ cup milk

Stir together flour, sugar, baking powder, and salt. Cut in butter till crumbly. Combine egg and milk; add all at once to dry ingredients. Stir just till all dry ingredients are moistened. Continue as directed in recipe.

Fresh Fruit Crisp

½ cup quick-cooking rolled oats
½ cup packed brown sugar
¼ cup all-purpose flour
½ teaspoon ground cinnamon
Dash salt
¼ cup butter *or* margarine
5 cups sliced peeled peaches, apples, *or* pears
Vanilla ice cream *or* light cream

Combine oats, brown sugar, flour, cinnamon, and salt; cut in butter till mixture is crumbly. Set aside.

Place fruit in a 10x6x2-inch baking dish. Sprinkle oat mixture over fruit. Bake, uncovered, at 350° till fruit is tender, about 40 minutes. Serve warm with ice cream or light cream. Makes 6 servings.

Fine examples of casserole desserts, *Cheese-Baked Apples* and *Cranberry-Peach Cobbler* are made with fresh fruits. These colorful meal-cappers go together with very little effort.

Fresh Strawberry Cobbler

Cobbler Topper (see page 88)
⅔ **cup sugar**
2 **tablespoons cornstarch**
1½ **cups water**
4 **cups fresh strawberries**
1 **teaspoon vanilla**
1 **tablespoon sugar**
Vanilla ice cream

Prepare Cobbler Topper; set aside. In saucepan combine the ⅔ cup sugar and cornstarch. Stir in water; cook and stir till thickened and bubbly. Cut any large berries in half. Add berries to mixture in saucepan; cook and stir till bubbly, about 5 minutes longer. Stir in vanilla.

Turn into a 2-quart casserole. Drop topper into 8 mounds atop *hot* fruit. Sprinkle with the 1 tablespoon sugar. Bake, uncovered, at 425° till lightly browned, about 25 minutes. Serve warm with ice cream. Makes 8 servings.

Apple and Raisin Cobbler

Cobbler Topper (see page 88)
½ **cup packed brown sugar**
2 **tablespoons cornstarch**
¼ **teaspoon ground ginger**
1¼ **cups water**
¼ **cup raisins**
6 **cups sliced peeled apples**
1 **tablespoon lemon juice**
1 **tablespoon butter *or* margarine**
1 **tablespoon granulated sugar**
Vanilla ice cream

Prepare Cobbler Topper; set aside. In saucepan combine the brown sugar, cornstarch, and ginger. Stir in water and raisins. Cook and stir till thickened and bubbly. Stir in apples, lemon juice, and butter. Cook till apples are hot, about 5 minutes. Turn into a 2-quart casserole.

Drop topper into 8 mounds atop *hot* fruit. Sprinkle with the granulated sugar. Bake, uncovered, at 425° till lightly browned, about 20 minutes. Serve warm with vanilla ice cream. Makes 8 servings.

Peach-Pecan Dessert (pictured on page 76)

1 **30-ounce can peach slices**
¼ **cup sugar**
2 **tablespoons cornstarch**
¼ **teaspoon salt**
1 **tablespoon lemon juice**
Few drops almond extract
2 **egg whites**
¼ **teaspoon cream of tartar**
¼ **teaspoon ground cinnamon**
¼ **cup sugar**
2 **egg yolks**
¼ **cup all-purpose flour**
¼ **cup chopped pecans**

Drain peaches, reserving syrup. In saucepan stir together ¼ cup sugar, cornstarch, and salt. Stir in reserved syrup; cook and stir till thickened and bubbly. Remove from heat; stir in lemon juice and almond extract. Set aside a few peach slices for garnish; stir remaining into hot mixture. Set aside.

Beat egg whites with cream of tartar and cinnamon till soft peaks form, about 1 minute. Gradually add ¼ cup sugar, beating till stiff peaks form, about 3 minutes. Beat egg yolks till thick and lemon-colored, about 4 minutes. Fold yolks into whites; fold in flour.

Return peach mixture in saucepan to boiling; turn into a 1½-quart casserole. Immediately top *hot* fruit with batter, spreading evenly to edges. Sprinkle with pecans. Bake, uncovered, at 350° till done, about 40 minutes. Garnish with reserved peach slices. Makes 6 servings.

Elegant Fruit Combo

1 **16-ounce can peach halves**
1 **cup fresh cranberries**
¼ **cup sugar**
1 **large banana, sliced**
1 **pint vanilla ice cream**

Drain peaches, reserving syrup. Place peach halves in a bowl; cover and set aside. In a 1-quart casserole stir together reserved peach syrup, cranberries, and sugar. Bake, covered, at 350° for 1¼ hours.

To serve, stir reserved peach halves and banana slices into cranberry mixture. Top each serving with a scoop of vanilla ice cream. Makes 6 servings.

Citus Crunch Dessert

1 cup all-purpose flour
⅓ cup packed brown sugar
½ cup butter *or* margarine
1 cup quick-cooking
   rolled oats
¼ cup flaked coconut
⅓ cup granulated sugar
1 tablespoon cornstarch
½ of a 6-ounce can frozen
   orange juice
   concentrate, thawed
   (6 tablespoons)
1 16-ounce can orange and
   grapefruit sections
   Vanilla ice cream

Combine flour and brown sugar. Cut in butter till mixture resembles fine crumbs; stir in oats and coconut. Pat *half* the crumb mixture evenly into an 8x8x2-inch baking pan; set remaining crumb mixture aside.

In saucepan combine granulated sugar and cornstarch; blend in juice concentrate. Drain fruit, reserving syrup. Add reserved syrup to cornstarch mixture. Cook and stir till thickened and bubbly; stir in fruit.

Pour fruit mixture atop crumb mixture in pan; sprinkle with reserved crumbs. Bake, uncovered, at 350° for 30 to 35 minutes. Serve warm with ice cream, if desired. Serves 6.

Bittersweet Chocolate Soufflé

3 egg yolks
2 tablespoons butter *or*
   margarine
2 tablespoons all-purpose
   flour
¼ teaspoon salt
¾ cup milk
2 1-ounce squares
   unsweetened chocolate,
   melted and cooled
¼ cup sugar
2 tablespoons hot water
3 egg whites
½ teaspoon vanilla
¼ cup sugar
   Sweetened whipped cream

In small bowl beat egg yolks till thick and lemon-colored, about 4 minutes; set aside. In saucepan melt butter; stir in flour and salt. Add milk all at once; cook and stir till thickened and bubbly.

Stir *half* the hot mixture into beaten egg yolks; mix well. Return to hot mixture in saucepan; cook and stir 2 minutes more. Remove from heat. Stir together cooled chocolate, ¼ cup sugar, and hot water. Stir chocolate mixture into egg mixture; set aside.

Beat egg whites and vanilla till soft peaks form, about 1 minute. Gradually add ¼ cup sugar, beating till stiff peaks form, about 3 minutes. Fold into chocolate mixture.

Turn into an ungreased 1½-quart soufflé dish. Bake, uncovered, at 325° till knife inserted just off-center comes out clean, 55 to 60 minutes. Serve immediately with sweetened whipped cream. Makes 6 servings.

Rich Rice Pudding

2 cups milk
½ cup regular rice
½ cup raisins
¼ cup butter *or* margarine
2 cups milk
3 beaten eggs
⅓ cup sugar
1 teaspoon vanilla
½ teaspoon salt
   Ground cinnamon
   Light cream

In heavy 2-quart saucepan bring 2 cups milk, rice, and raisins to boiling; reduce heat. Cover; cook over very low heat till rice is tender, about 15 minutes. Remove from heat; stir in butter or margarine till melted.

In bowl combine 2 cups milk, eggs, sugar, vanilla, and salt. Gradually stir rice mixture into egg mixture. Pour into a 10x6x2-inch baking dish.

Bake, uncovered, at 325° for 30 minutes. Stir; sprinkle with cinnamon. Bake till knife inserted halfway between center and edge comes out clean, about 20 minutes more. Serve warm or chilled with cream. Makes 6 servings.

Ginger-Lemon Pudding Cake

1⅓ **cups all-purpose flour**
½ **cup packed brown sugar**
1 **tablespoon baking powder**
1 **teaspoon ground cinnamon**
½ **teaspoon salt**
½ **teaspoon ground ginger**
½ **cup water**
¼ **cup light molasses**
¼ **cup cooking oil**
⅓ **cup chopped nuts**
½ **cup packed brown sugar**
½ **of a 6-ounce can frozen
      lemonade concentrate, thawed
      (6 tablespoons)
      Vanilla ice cream**

Stir together flour, ½ cup brown sugar, baking powder, cinnamon, salt, and ginger. Combine the ½ cup water, molasses, and oil. Stir into dry ingredients till nearly smooth; fold in nuts. Turn into an ungreased 8x8x2-inch baking dish.

Bring 1½ cups water to boiling; stir in ½ cup brown sugar and lemonade concentrate. Pour carefully over batter in baking dish. Bake, uncovered, at 350° till done, 40 to 45 minutes. Serve warm with ice cream. Serves 6.

Microwave cooking directions: Stir together flour, ½ cup brown sugar, baking powder, cinnamon, salt, and ginger. Combine the ½ cup water, molasses, and oil. Stir into dry ingredients till nearly smooth; fold in nuts. Turn into an ungreased 8x8x2-inch nonmetal baking dish.

In a 4-cup glass measure combine 1⅔ cups water, ½ cup brown sugar, and lemonade concentrate. Cook, uncovered, in countertop microwave oven till boiling, 4 to 5 minutes. Carefully pour over batter in baking dish. Micro-cook, uncovered, till top springs back when touched with finger, about 8 minutes, giving dish ¼ turn every 2 minutes.

Baked Pumpkin Pudding

6 **tablespoons butter *or*
      margarine**
¾ **cup packed brown sugar**
¼ **cup granulated sugar**
2 **eggs**
1½ **cups all-purpose flour**
½ **teaspoon salt**
½ **teaspoon baking soda**
½ **teaspoon ground cinnamon**
½ **teaspoon ground ginger**
¼ **teaspoon ground nutmeg**
¾ **cup mashed cooked pumpkin
      or canned pumpkin**
½ **cup buttermilk**
½ **cup chopped walnuts**

Cream butter and sugars together till light; beat in eggs. Stir together flour, salt, soda, cinnamon, ginger, and nutmeg. Combine pumpkin and buttermilk; add to creamed mixture alternately with dry ingredients, mixing well after each addition. Fold in chopped walnuts.

Spoon mixture into a greased and floured 6½-cup ring mold; cover tightly with foil. Bake at 350° for 1 hour. Let stand 10 minutes. Unmold. Serve with whipped cream, if desired. Makes 12 to 16 servings.

Apple Bread Pudding

3 **cups dry bread cubes
      (4 slices)**
1½ **cups applesauce**
⅛ **teaspoon ground cinnamon
      Dash ground nutmeg**
2 **tablespoons butter *or*
      margarine**
2 **cups milk**
2 **beaten eggs**
½ **cup sugar**
½ **teaspoon vanilla
      Dash salt
      Ground cinnamon**

In a buttered 8x8x2-inch baking pan layer *half* the dry bread cubes. Combine applesauce, the ⅛ teaspoon cinnamon, and nutmeg. Spread applesauce mixture over bread cubes. Layer remaining bread cubes atop; dot with butter.

Combine milk, eggs, sugar, vanilla, and salt. Pour over bread mixture. Lightly sprinkle cinnamon over top. Bake, uncovered, at 350° till knife inserted just off-center comes out clean, 55 to 60 minutes. Makes 6 servings.

Index

P-R